Lent with
New Da

The Bible Reading Fellowship
15 The Chambers, Vineyard
Abingdon OX14 3FE
brf.org.uk

The Bible Reading Fellowship (BRF) is a Registered Charity (233280)

ISBN 978 0 85746 788 1
All rights reserved

This edition © The Bible Reading Fellowship 2018
Cover image © Thinkstock

Distributed in Australia by:
MediaCom Education Inc, PO Box 610, Unley, SA 5061
Tel: 1 800 811 311 | admin@mediacom.org.au

Distributed in New Zealand by:
Scripture Union Wholesale, PO Box 760, Wellington
Tel: 04 385 0421 | suwholesale@clear.net.nz

Acknowledgements
Scripture quotations marked NRSV are taken from The New Revised Standard Version
of the Bible, Anglicised Edition, copyright © 1989, 1995 by the Division of Christian
Education of the National Council of the Churches of Christ in the USA. Used by
permission. All rights reserved.

Scipture quotations marked NIV are taken from The Holy Bible, New International
Version, Anglicised edition, copyright © 1979, 1984, 2011 by Biblica. Used by
permission of Hodder & Stoughton Publishers, an Hachette UK company. All rights
reserved. 'NIV' is a registered trademark of Biblica. UK trademark number 1448790.

A catalogue record for this book is available from the British Library

Printed by Gutenberg Press, Tarxien, Malta

Lent with
New Daylight

Edited by **Sally Welch**   **Lent 2019**

About the contributors

Margaret Silf is an ecumenical Christian committed to working across and beyond traditional divisions. She is the author of a number of books for 21st-century spiritual pilgrims and is a retreat facilitator.

Liz Hoare is an ordained Anglican priest and teaches spiritual formation at Wycliffe Hall, Oxford. Her interests lie in the history and literature of Christian spirituality and their connections with today's world. She is married to Toddy, a priest and sculptor, and they have a teenage son.

Michael Mitton works freelance in the areas of spirituality and mission. He is also an Honorary Canon of Derby Cathedral and is the NSM Priest in Charge of St Paul's Derby. He is author of *Travellers of the Heart* (BRF, 2013).

Naomi Starkey is a curate in the Church in Wales, working in Welsh and English across six rural churches on the Llyn Peninsula. She previously worked as a BRF commissioning editor from 1997 to 2015 and has written a number of books, including *The Recovery of Joy* (BRF, 2017) and *The Recovery of Hope* (BRF, 2016).

Introduction

As regular readers of *New Daylight* will be aware, my personal spiritual practice is based around pilgrimage. The spirituality of pilgrimage – broadly defined as 'a spiritual journey to a sacred place' – and its disciplines can be extended out from the actual physical journey into all aspects of everyday life and prayer, offering insights from the road that apply equally well at 'home', whatever that may be.

One of the most wonderful and challenging things about pilgrimage is how much time you have to spend with yourself. All your preoccupations, all your busyness that takes you from one activity to the next, are stripped away, and you are left with the basic necessities of travelling to the next place of food or shelter. Even if you do not journey alone, there will be times when you have run out of things to say and you simply walk along, each member of the party immersed in their own thoughts, face-to-face with their true selves, perhaps for the first time in many years.

It is for a similar reason that I like the period of Lent, the 40 days before Easter, a time traditionally set aside for those preparing for baptism on Easter Eve. These people would, as part of their final preparation, leave behind all the things of this world that got in the way of their relationship with God. They spent time in fasting, prayer, serving the poor and other disciplines of the Christian life. They went through final instruction in what being a Christian was all about. They prepared for lives of loving service in the world.

So may we take up this ancient tradition and use Lent as a time for renewing our relationship with God, stripping away all that has accumulated around our souls – the distractions with which the world has surrounded us – and preparing to rediscover who we are as God's people.

We are called to face our fears and our failures with courage and dignity, relying on God's love and mercy. We are called to be God's children once again.

Lent begins with Ash Wednesday – a serious day. Of all the days in the church calendar, it is the one that most invites us to inner reflection and self-examination. Ash Wednesday encourages us to look at the pattern of our lives, to make space for God and to re-engage once more with prayer and study, if this has been lacking, or to extend and deepen our practice if we already incorporate these into our daily lives. We are invited to take a good, hard look at our relationship with God and with our neighbours and to repent and turn away from any destructive ways into which we have fallen, in order to train ourselves into new habits. At the threshold of this time of reappraisal and examination, let us expect transformation and a deepening of understanding of the Christian way.

As we begin this Lenten Bible study, we will be helped in our reflection not only by the writing of the authors, but also by a series of questions that they have framed in order to direct our minds and help us engage with the issues their studies are highlighting.

We focus first on the practice of contemplative prayer, introduced to us by Margaret Silf. She offers, through her reflections and prayers, guidance on how we might incorporate this practice into our own lives, and shows us how our knowledge of God might grow deeper through a pattern of silence and meditation.

We continue our Lenten journey with Liz Hoare and Michael Mitton, who lead us through studies of place and 'non-place' or exile. Through their writing, we are encouraged to examine the importance of place in our own lives, and what it might mean to be 'in exile' today.

Finally, we walk the road to Easter in the company of Naomi Starkey, as she explores what it means to 'understand' the life and message of Christ in ourselves and in the lives of those around us.

As you journey through Lent in the company of these wise and experienced writers, I pray that you will find the help and support you need to make a good and holy Lent, preparing yourself in your heart and mind and soul for that most joyous festival of Easter.

Heavenly Father, grant that through our prayers and study this Lenten season we may enter more fully into the joy of Easter, with hearts and minds prepared to celebrate the mystery of your love. Amen.

What do you hope to gain from this Lent study?
How will it fit into the pattern of your daily life?

Sally Ann Welch

See pages 72–73 for suggestions for how to use this material in a group setting.

Lent study reflections

Contemplative prayer

I walk regularly around my own neighbourhood and know every path and tree along the way, but familiarity, I realise, can make me blind. So every so often I say to myself, 'Suppose you didn't live here, but were just visiting. Look at these paths, these trees, as though you were here for the first time in this present moment. Listen to the birds you hear every morning, and hear them for the first time.' Then I see everything with fresh eyes. I appreciate what I see. I even say 'thank you' for it.

Contemplative prayer is rather like this. It can help us see the world, and the people around us, in a fresh light, revealing the extraordinary within the ordinary and turning our garden hedges into burning bushes. It can open our inner eyes to see more deeply into the mystery of things – to tune in to the pulse of God throbbing through all creation.

I once visited a wild and beautiful place on a remote Scottish island, where sea eagles make their homes. It was easy in such a location to feel close to the divine mystery. Afterwards, in a gift shop, I discovered that someone else had also experienced this sense of the entire wonder of life present in every single part. I found an unusual painting: a perfect image of a sea eagle painted on a feather not more than 10cm long – the whole eagle revealed on one of its feathers. What an amazing piece of art, and what a perfect reminder that the whole of the divine mystery is present in every part of creation.

To enter into contemplative prayer, we need to come to silence and stillness, adjusting our life's pace to the much slower heartbeat of eternity. In an age that demands rapid results and fast fixes, this is countercultural. In a culture that prefers to take an instant harvest from the supermarket shelves, the task of contemplation is the patient preparation of the ground of our hearts for spiritual seeding, so that God can do the growing.

I hope these days of exploration may help you slow down your heart's clock, that you might feel the pulse of the divine presence, moment by moment, sustaining your life's journey.

MARGARET SILF

At home in God's heart

How lovely is your dwelling place, O Lord of hosts! My soul longs, indeed it faints for the courts of the Lord; my heart and my flesh sing for joy to the living God. Even the sparrow finds a home, and the swallow a nest for herself, where she may lay her young, at your altars, O Lord of hosts, my King and my God. Happy are those who live in your house, ever singing your praise.

We can learn contemplation from the humblest of God's creatures. I discovered this one morning on mainland Orkney off the north coast of Scotland, where I was visiting the 5,000-year-old Neolithic chambered cairn at Maeshowe.

The guide led us across the fields and through a low entrance gap into the ancient inner chamber. Human life had ebbed and flowed here through five millennia, its passing celebrated in hallowed ritual, and an awed silence fell as we breathed in the atmosphere of this sacred space.

Silence, that is, except for the occasional rustle of wings, as a mother swallow circled the chamber around her family of chicks, apparently oblivious to our intrusion. She had built her nest in the place that would have been the focal point of the rituals once performed there, and ever since, the guide told us, she was always there in the chamber, focusing on what mattered most – the raising of her brood. She was surely one of God's natural contemplatives, with everything to teach us.

A key component of contemplative prayer is the art of focusing. Some people use a familiar word or phrase, such as 'Maranatha' or 'Come, Lord Jesus', to help themselves come to a focused inner stillness. Others let their gaze rest on an object, such as a flower, or a sacred symbol or image. This keeps the normally over-busy conscious mind peacefully occupied, and allows us to enter a deeper stillness, just as I entered the ancient stillness of the cairn that morning. But it was the swallow who taught me more than any prayer manual could have done. She knew what mattered most, and she allowed nothing to distract her from her holy task.

May my heart stay in orbit around what matters most,
wherever my mind may wander.

MARGARET SILF

Basking in the light

The Lord spoke to Moses, saying: Speak to Aaron and his sons, saying, Thus you shall bless the Israelites: You shall say to them, The Lord bless you and keep you; the Lord make his face to shine upon you, and be gracious to you; the Lord lift up his countenance upon you, and give you peace. So they shall put my name on the Israelites, and I will bless them.

A story is told about a man who used to go into his local church when all was quiet and simply sit at the back and gaze straight ahead. The pastor noticed this and began to wonder whether this silent visitor might be seeking help. One morning he approached the man and asked him gently, 'Is there anything I can do for you?' The man looked up in some surprise and said, 'Thank you, but there is nothing I need. I love to come in here and sit still and I just look at him, and he looks at me.'

This is contemplative prayer – just sitting, gazing into the heart of the mystery and letting the mystery gaze back upon us. No words needed. Today's reading invites us simply to let the light of God shine upon us, bringing grace, peace and blessing. A big ask – yet all we have to do is to let it shine.

If you live in a climate where the sun rarely shines, you will know how eagerly we go out and bask in it when it does, wanting nothing more than simply to soak up the warmth and the light. In countries in the throes of drought, people rush outside when the precious rain falls, just for the joy of being exposed to the life-giving water soaking down to the roots of their being.

Contemplative prayer is rather like this – simply basking in the warmth and light of God's love, simply letting ourselves be drenched in life-sustaining, life-restoring grace.

Quakers speak of prayer as 'holding someone in the light'. No need to verbalise our problems or tell God what needs to be done. Enough just to be held in the light.

To be blessed by God is as simple as letting ourselves bask in the light of God's love.

MARGARET SILF

11

Windows into mystery

Surely, this commandment that I am commanding you today is not too hard for you, nor is it too far away. It is not in heaven, that you should say, 'Who will go up to heaven for us, and get it for us so that we may hear it and observe it?' Neither is it beyond the sea, that you should say, 'Who will cross to the other side of the sea for us, and get it for us so that we may hear it and observe it?' No, the word is very near to you; it is in your mouth and in your heart for you to observe.

At this time of the year readers in the northern hemisphere can look out at the natural world and see the deciduous trees still closed up in the sleep of winter. Soon the new buds will sprout and the branches gradually transform into springtime green. As the temperature rises, the flowers will emerge, and, in the fullness of time, the fruits. If we had never seen this miracle before, could we believe that all this new life is already there inside the tree that looks so lifeless?

And suppose we found caterpillars eating our cabbages in the garden, and someone were to tell us that there is a butterfly inside each one of them. Would we believe it? If we didn't know the whole story, wouldn't we think that maybe the leaves, flowers and fruit were deposited on the tree by some outside agency? Would we not think that the butterfly had flown in from some exotic land?

Contemplative prayer opens a window into that deep interior, inviting us to catch a glimpse of the fruit inside the tree, the butterfly inside the caterpillar and, most amazingly, the fullness of the kingdom of God latent inside our own hearts, awaiting the fullness of time, and grace, for its flowering. We can't force it. We can't even imagine it. But we are invited to believe in it, and to nourish it in the silence of contemplation – the seed-bed and the nursery of divine transformation.

May we learn to stop our frantic search for the kingdom, so that we can become still and know its reality deep within us and all around us.

MARGARET SILF

Rooted in God

Happy are those who do not follow the advice of the wicked, or take the path that sinners tread, or sit in the seat of scoffers; but their delight is in the law of the Lord, and on his law they meditate day and night. They are like trees planted by streams of water, which yield their fruit in its season, and their leaves do not wither. In all that they do, they prosper.

Trees are great teachers. Among many other things we learn from them, as in today's reading, is the fact of the intimate connection between the roots and branches, each depending on the other for the fullness of life. This surely applies not just to trees but also in our own lives. The branches of our outer lives can never thrive if the roots of our inner lives are not planted deep in the soil that both sustains them and gives them stability and a place of belonging.

The psalmist reveals that the tree whose roots go deep into the living water will survive the dry seasons and bring forth leaves and fruit in due time. Those whose lives are planted in God will likewise bear spiritual fruit.

This connection reminds me of an oil lamp. One end of the wick must be immersed in the oil and the other end extended into the world, otherwise there will be no light. The same is true for us. Our lives, ideally, are both contemplative and active. If they are to bear fruit, we must ensure that our hearts remain immersed in God, while our lives also branch out into the world, bearing fruit. All contemplation and no action means that, however faithful and intense our prayer, it will not find expression in the wider world. All action and no contemplation means that any fruit our lives might bear will quickly wither for lack of deep sustenance.

Happy the pilgrim who, like the tree in the psalm, finds a balance between contemplation and action, for that pilgrim's life shall bear fruit that will nourish a spiritually starving world.

May our deep invisible roots remain immersed in the ocean of God's love, so that the branches of our lives may survive the drought and bear fruit for the nations.

MARGARET SILF

The gift of the dewfall

I will heal their disloyalty; I will love them freely, for my anger has turned from them. I will be like the dew to Israel; he shall blossom like the lily, he shall strike root like the forests of Lebanon. His shoots shall spread out; his beauty shall be like the olive tree, and his fragrance like that of Lebanon. They shall again live beneath my shadow, they shall flourish as a garden; they shall blossom like the vine, their fragrance shall be like the wine of Lebanon.

'Dew' is a beautiful, gentle word. In today's reading God promises to fall like dew upon Israel. And the result will be a blossoming forth and fruitful flourishing, and the emergence of fresh new growth from deep roots, as far-reaching and majestic as the forests of Lebanon.

I was once visiting the cemetery of a convent in south Wales, reflecting on the life of a sister whom I knew and who had recently died and been buried there. It was early morning and the rising sun shone down, causing the dewdrops on the grass to shine like diamonds.

It felt to me at that moment that God was offering me a diamond in a dewdrop and, with that, the sense of an invitation to make a choice: what would I prefer, if I could choose – a precious, sparkling diamond or a precious, sparkling dewdrop?

My response to this unspoken question was clear. I would choose the dewdrop. The diamond would, of course, be very valuable and very beautiful, while a dewdrop would be gone by midday. However, the dewdrop would, by midday, have soaked deep into the dry earth and helped to make it a little bit more fruitful. I wanted my life to be like that. Contemplative prayer is like this – not a gem to be kept in a showcase, but a drop of life itself, soaking into our hearts and bringing forth new growth.

Diamonds may be a girl's (and boy's) best friend, but a drop of dew carries the source of life itself. When it comes to a choice, really there is no contest.

May the presence and power of God soak deep into our hearts like dew and grow shoots of love and compassion in our lives.

MARGARET SILF

Burning bushes in the park

Moses was keeping the flock of his father-in-law Jethro, the priest of Midian; he led his flock beyond the wilderness, and came to Horeb, the mountain of God. There the angel of the Lord appeared to him in a flame of fire out of a bush; he looked, and the bush was blazing, yet it was not consumed. Then Moses said, 'I must turn aside and look at this great sight, and see why the bush is not burned up.' When the Lord saw that he had turned aside to see, God called to him out of the bush, 'Moses, Moses!' And he said, 'Here I am.' Then he said, 'Come no closer! Remove the sandals from your feet, for the place on which you are standing is holy ground.'

One of my favourite photographs of my daughter was taken when she was just a baby, at the local garden centre, where for a few minutes she lay in her pram gazing up at a fuchsia flower with totally rapt attention. She was seeing her first fuchsia. She could have been the very first person ever to see a fuchsia and be overwhelmed by the wonder and beauty of it. She was on holy ground, and somewhere in her infant heart she knew it.

When babies are caught up in a moment of wonder like this, nothing else exists for them. Their hearts and minds are still unburdened by all the baggage they will accumulate along life's way. Such moments are timeless, when there is no past to regret, no fear for the future. Moses has plenty to regret and even more to fear, yet his wonder overcomes everything as he stands in awe before the burning bush and knows that he stands on holy ground.

Contemplative prayer takes us to that eternal moment in the core of our being, when time stands still and our hearts are momentarily free of all the clutter, stilled into receptivity. Then we too can look into a flower and see eternity. We can walk through the park and see the blaze of glory in every bush.

May we know the wonder and joy of the timeless moments
that only the quietened, focused, contemplative heart can receive,
and only God can give.

MARGARET SILF

Connecting earth and heaven

Jacob left Beer-sheba and went towards Haran. He came to a certain place and stayed there for the night, because the sun had set. Taking one of the stones of the place, he put it under his head and lay down in that place. And he dreamed that there was a ladder set up on the earth, the top of it reaching to heaven; and the angels of God were ascending and descending on it... Then Jacob woke from his sleep and said, 'Surely the Lord is in this place – and I did not know it!'

Today we are given a little vignette from a hard and stony journey as Jacob makes his weary way towards Haran. Night falls. All he has is the rocky ground and a stone for a pillow – hardly the setting for calm contemplation. However, part of the secret of contemplation is to allow ourselves to be drawn into those layers of heart and soul that lie below the level of the conscious mind. Prayer can lead us there, as can music, poetry, the natural world and, of course, the gift of sleep. Ironically, it is in the darkness of sleep that Jacob finds the gift of enlightenment.

Our unconscious minds often communicate their wisdom through symbols. Jacob's ladder is a wonderful example. It also teaches us that authentic contemplative prayer can connect heaven and earth. It opens our hearts to recognise the many ways in which our daily lived experience, even at its hardest, can be suffused with the glory of God.

True contemplative prayer is not a withdrawal from everyday life, but a deeper immersion into it. It invites us to go deep within, to find God at the core of our being, and then to return to our everyday lives, bringing with us the heart knowledge that everything we do and everything we are has its source and its destiny in God. It takes us, for a timeless moment, to the top of the heavenly ladder, and then calls us to return to the place on earth and proclaim, with Jacob, that 'the Lord is in this place – and I did not know it!'

May we recognise the presence of God along the stony paths
as well as in the consolations of prayer.

MARGARET SILF

Emptiness transformed

On the third day there was a wedding in Cana of Galilee, and the mother of Jesus was there. Jesus and his disciples had also been invited to the wedding. When the wine gave out… his mother said to the servants, 'Do whatever he tells you.' Now standing there were six stone water-jars for the Jewish rites of purification, each holding twenty or thirty gallons. Jesus said to them, 'Fill the jars with water.' And they filled them up to the brim. He said to them, 'Now draw some out and take it to the chief steward.'

The miracle at Cana could be a textbook exercise in the practice of contemplative prayer. We are all familiar with the story of Jesus' first miracle. The phrase 'turning water into wine' has become a cliché, used by many who have never read the original story.

This story of transformation, however, is also almost a step-by-step guide to contemplation. The first, most crucial stage of the process is emptiness. The wine has given out. Mary is the first to notice this and make Jesus aware of the crisis, and when the wine runs out in the middle of a wedding feast, there really is a crisis, at least at the human level.

Contemplative prayer also begins with emptiness, but because our minds are so constantly occupied with minor and major matters, we need to learn certain techniques for emptying them, for clearing out the clutter, perhaps by using a mantra or familiar phrase to still ourselves and, as it were, put our unruly thoughts aside, into a playpen, so that our hearts can focus on the desire to go deeper into God.

Into this situation of emptiness Jesus issues the call to fill up the vessels with the water needed for cleansing. We too are invited to come to stillness and allow the muddy waters of our minds to settle, leaving clear water in its place.

Only then can the transformation happen. The water at Cana becomes wine. The water of our daily lives is transformed through grace into the wine of a life lived in God.

May we have the grace to let ourselves be emptied out, the patience to await the settling of our souls and the joy of tasting the wine.

MARGARET SILF

A question of priorities

Now as they went on their way, he entered a certain village, where a woman named Martha welcomed him into her home. She had a sister named Mary, who sat at the Lord's feet and listened to what he was saying. But Martha was distracted by her many tasks; so she came to him and asked, 'Lord, do you not care that my sister has left me to do all the work by myself? Tell her then to help me.' But the Lord answered her, 'Martha, Martha, you are worried and distracted by many things; there is need of only one thing. Mary has chosen the better part, which will not be taken away from her.'

When I let my imagination rove over this story I see an exhausted Jesus, looking for a time of rest. Everyone wants a piece of him, and right now what he longs for is some peace and quiet. He has a bolthole with his dear friends in Bethany. They welcome him warmly as always, and Martha bustles around in the kitchen, preparing a meal for them. Mary meanwhile sits at Jesus' feet, and they share the quiet conversation of trusted friends.

I guess many readers feel a lot of sympathy with Martha. Hospitality, after all, is a sacred duty, and everyone wants a meal. So how do we feel about Jesus' apparent favouring of Mary in this situation? Perhaps it has something to tell us about the value of contemplation.

I wonder whether this story is less about favouring one sister's choice over that of the other but rather an invitation to reflect on our priorities. The meal is important, but there are some things that are even more important. We might almost hear Jesus murmuring quietly to Martha, as he draws her lovingly into his presence and invites her to sit beside her sister, 'Martha, first things first.'

There is a Martha and Mary in each of us. Our inner Martha does need to attend to the practical life, but our inner Mary also needs to sit quietly in the presence of God. Sometimes it is a matter of priorities.

There is a time for work and a time for prayer. May we learn to honour each in its right time.

MARGARET SILF

Non-transferable grace

'Ten bridesmaids took their lamps and went to meet the bridegroom. Five of them were foolish, and five were wise. When the foolish took their lamps, they took no oil with them; but the wise took flasks of oil with their lamps... At midnight there was a shout, "Look! Here is the bridegroom! Come out to meet him." Then all those bridesmaids got up and trimmed their lamps. The foolish said to the wise, "Give us some of your oil, for our lamps are going out." But the wise replied, "No! There will not be enough for you and for us; you had better go to the dealers and buy some for yourselves."'

I once heard someone say, 'When I miss prayer for a day, God notices. When I miss prayer for a week, I notice. When I miss prayer for a month, everyone notices.' The energy we tap into in contemplation makes a difference. We carry it with us through our day-to-day living, just as the wise bridesmaids carry the spare oil for their lamps. An hour's contemplation is a gift in itself, but it also supplies the spiritual energy for all the hours ahead, when daily life will make its heavy demands on us. We can walk through our day assured that our spiritual flasks are well topped-up.

What do we make of the refusal of the wise bridesmaids to share their oil with their less mindful sisters? Is it a bit mean-spirited? When we apply this story to the practice of contemplation, we see one very important thing: the energy and grace that is given in prayer is non-transferable. Each of us has to find our own pathway into prayer. Certainly the fruits of that prayer can and do nourish many more people than ourselves, because they change the way we relate to the world around us. The heart that is anchored in God through prayer will always bear fruit for many and in all seasons, like the tree planted by the water. But each of us is individually responsible for making our own journey to the well of contemplation.

May we have the grace to take responsibility for our own contemplative journey and then generously share its fruits with all those who have need of them.

MARGARET SILF

A place apart

'And whenever you pray, do not be like the hypocrites; for they love to stand and pray in the synagogues and at the street corners, so that they may be seen by others. Truly I tell you, they have received their reward. But whenever you pray, go into your room and shut the door and pray to your Father who is in secret; and your Father who sees in secret will reward you. When you are praying, do not heap up empty phrases as the Gentiles do; for they think that they will be heard because of their many words.'

On a busy flight from Glasgow to Dubai a quiet young woman with a boisterous toddler sat across the aisle from me. For the first two hours she tended the child patiently until he finally fell asleep, his head on her lap. I assumed she would now relax. Instead she turned towards the window and the black night beyond, her hands folded in prayer. Half an hour later, she turned back, ran her hand lovingly over the child's sleeping head and returned to reading her magazine.

It was a powerful lesson about going to a still place and shutting the door. At the time we were flying directly over war-torn Iraq. Her quiet contemplation hovered like a blessing over the killing fields beneath us.

Today, at the beginning of Lent, we might pause to ask ourselves where, in today's frenzied world, we find our own inner space to go to, closing the door for a while against the daily demands of life. I have a friend who lives in an overcrowded flat in a deprived urban area. Her inner room is the view from her window of a tree growing on a patch of waste ground. That tree, in all its seasons, is her focal point, her doorway into contemplation.

Ash Wednesday is a doorway into a special time of reflection. How might we begin our Lenten journey by stepping through that doorway into a daily quiet space, trusting that the Father who sees all that happens in the secrecy of our souls meets us wherever we turn in our search for the holy mystery?

As Lent begins, may we meet God each day in our heart's wordless silence.

MARGARET SILF

No instructions needed

He also said, 'The kingdom of God is as if someone would scatter seed on the ground, and would sleep and rise night and day, and the seed would sprout and grow, he does not know how. The earth produces of itself, first the stalk, then the head, then the full grain in the head. But when the grain is ripe, at once he goes in with his sickle, because the harvest has come.'

The simple act of sowing a seed is an act of faith. We drop a tiny speck of potential life into the cold earth, cover it up and let it disappear out of sight, and perhaps out of mind. The results may well surprise us as unexpected shoots and flowers emerge from that same cold earth a few months later.

To sow a seed, all that is needed is to tear open the seed packet and empty the contents into the ground. It would not occur to us to plant the seed packet along with the seed. The seed doesn't need any instructions about how and where it should be sown, how tall it will become or what it will look like when it blooms.

Contemplative prayer is a bit like that. It takes us into the depths of our being, where God is indwelling. We place ourselves into that stillness. The rest can safely be left to God. Our prayer doesn't need to give God any instructions as to how it should be answered. It doesn't need to include a wish list for all the blooms that we want our seed to produce.

Today's reading is a powerful reminder that prayer has an energy of its own. Time spent in stillness with God will sprout and grow in ways we do not understand and cannot necessarily see. It will flourish in its own way and its own time, without our help. We don't need to give it any instructions, nor should we dig it up to see how it is growing. Our only task is to gather the harvest in due season and share it with God's world.

May we learn to trust God more than we trust ourselves, as we sow our seeds of contemplation in the soil of God's infinite presence.

MARGARET SILF

In the eye of the storm

A gale swept down on the lake, and the boat was filling with water, and they were in danger. They went to him and woke him up, shouting, 'Master, Master, we are perishing!' And he woke up and rebuked the wind and the raging waves; they ceased, and there was a calm. He said to them, 'Where is your faith?' They were afraid and amazed, and said to one another, 'Who then is this, that he commands even the winds and the water, and they obey him?'

I once witnessed a disturbing scene involving a furious outburst by one person in a group of several friends. So fierce was the firestorm that erupted that several of the group immediately removed themselves from the scene. I could completely understand why they did so. They were genuinely afraid. The force of the negative energy flowing from the person who was causing the storm was like lava from an erupting volcano.

But one young woman stayed in the midst of the furore. She didn't say anything or enter the fray in any way. She simply stood there, eyes closed, in quiet prayer. While most people fled from the fury, she held herself, still and steady, in the eye of the hurricane.

The incident reminded me vividly of the story in today's reading. Jesus' friends are panicking, terrified for their lives and helpless to withstand the force of the storm. If they could have fled the onslaught of the waves they would surely have done so, but there is nowhere to go. So they turn to Jesus in their distress.

Jesus, asleep in the boat, is actually the still point at the eye of the storm. Perhaps there is a lesson for us here about the power of contemplative prayer. It takes a special kind of courage to stand our ground in calm and quiet when the storms of life are swirling dangerously all around us. This story assures us that this still point is the only place from which real and lasting peace can ultimately flow. Our world needs this peace today as desperately as those on that beleaguered little boat in Galilee.

In contemplation may we discover that the stillness
is more powerful than the storm.

MARGARET SILF

Awake at sunrise

'Be dressed for action and have your lamps lit; be like those who are waiting for their master to return from the wedding banquet, so that they may open the door for him as soon as he comes and knocks. Blessed are those slaves whom the master finds alert when he comes; truly I tell you, he will fasten his belt and have them sit down to eat, and he will come and serve them. If he comes during the middle of the night, or near dawn, and finds them so, blessed are those slaves.'

A story is told of a spiritual guru who taught his followers various spiritual practices and methods of prayer and meditation. They in turn spent much time trying to put into practice the techniques they were learning from him. One day one of the students asked the guru, 'What can I do to achieve enlightenment?' The guru replied with another question, 'What can you do to make the sun rise?' The student, taken off guard by this unexpected response, admitted, 'There is nothing I can do to make the sun rise.' The guru smiled, 'And there is nothing you can do to achieve enlightenment.' Frustrated now, the student asked, a touch querulously, 'So why are you asking us to practise all these meditation techniques?' 'So that you will be awake when the sun rises,' replied the guru.

There are many different ways of practising prayer and contemplation. There is no one 'right' way, and no practice, if truly rooted in God, is 'wrong'. None of them delivers a finished product called 'enlightenment'. Each of them offers a particular way of preparing our hearts to recognise the glimpses of the divine presence when we encounter it, and to live in its light even when we don't see it.

We too, like the guru's students, can become so eager to grasp a light that still lies beyond the horizon of our understanding that we fail to engage with the daily disciplines that are preparing us to recognise the light when it dawns; so concerned with achieving 'nirvana' that we seek to bypass the practices that help us watch and wait for the master's coming.

We are not called to achieve anything, but to stay awake, hearts and minds prepared, receptive and alert, to welcome the dawning of God's new day.

MARGARET SILF

23

Place

Places are important to us as human beings for many reasons. There are places we have left and never wish to revisit, and there are places that are held dear in our heart even if we are now far removed from them. As embodied beings, we are confined to space and time and therefore places have meaning for us, for we are earthed in this world.

Throughout scripture God meets with people in different places, some of them already loaded with significance because of something that happened there. Thus Jerusalem, the holy city, was special to the Jewish nation as the place where God had his dwelling, the temple. This example is a reminder, however, of the ephemeral nature of places, for the time came when God's people were taken away into exile and the temple was destroyed. The people had to learn how to sing the Lord's song in a strange land, a place where God's name was not honoured. Most of the exiles did not expect him to show up there and had to learn that God is not confined to space and time and is present everywhere, waiting to come to all those who seek him.

Today we can theoretically go anywhere we please. In the west, at least, we have a mobile society, always on the move, restless and seeking new thrills in new places. Yet God is here, now, in the very places we find ourselves at this moment. What is more, he longs to make himself known. 'The word is very near to you; it is in your mouth and in your heart' (Deuteronomy 30:14, NRSV). The readings for the next two weeks explore how people met with God in different places. They frequently bear out the truth of the poet R.S. Thomas' words: 'You gave me only this small pool that the more I drink from, the more overflows me with sourceless light' ('The Gift'). They invite us to see with fresh eyes the places we have visited in the past and currently inhabit and say with Jacob at Bethel, 'Surely the Lord is in this place… This is none other than the house of God, and this is the gate of heaven' (Genesis 28:16–17, NRSV).

LIZ HOARE

The altar: the place where it began

[Abram] journeyed on by stages from the Negeb as far as Bethel, to the place where his tent had been at the beginning, between Bethel and Ai, to the place where he had made an altar at the first; and there Abram called on the name of the Lord.

It may seem strange to begin a series of Bible notes on 'place' with a wandering nomad retracing his steps, but Abram's return to the location where he first called on the name of the Lord was a vital reference point in his spiritual development. It was the place he had pitched his tent and built an altar, actions that marked the spot as significant for a physical and spiritual journey combined. The tent was packed away for the next phase of the journey, but that pile of stones remained as a sign that here Abram had communed with God.

The letter to the Hebrews tells us that when God first called Abram (Genesis 12:1), he set out 'not knowing where he was going' (Hebrews 11:8). This may sound irresponsible, especially to people who are used to travelling with a map and a destination, complete with good places to stop rest and refuelling, but Abram was learning to walk by faith and not by sight (2 Corinthians 5:7). His directions consisted of a promise from God that he would be shown a land full of blessing. So he, along with his family and possessions, journeyed from place to place, learning along the way.

Abram's walk of faith was not straightforward, however, and things went wrong in Egypt. How could Abram recover from this disastrous turn of events? Wisely, he went back to where he had heard God clearly and first found his bearings. Abram needed them, for almost immediately he faced a new challenge with his nephew Lot, but this time he acted with wisdom and discretion. The place where he had made an altar to the Lord became for Abram the place of regeneration and transformation.

Thank you, Lord, for the anchor points in my walk with you.
Help me to recall them in times of darkness. Amen

LIZ HOARE

Peniel: the place of wrestling

Jacob was left alone; and a man wrestled with him until daybreak. When the man saw that he did not prevail against Jacob, he struck him on the hip socket; and Jacob's hip was put out of joint as he wrestled with him. Then he said, 'Let me go, for the day is breaking.' But Jacob said, 'I will not let you go, unless you bless me.' So he said to him, 'What is your name?' And he said 'Jacob.' Then the man said, 'You shall no longer be called Jacob, but Israel, for you have striven with God and with humans, and have prevailed.'

I can recall walking down the lane close to where we lived in the darkness, shouting aloud to God about my situation. It is the closest I have come to a felt experience of wrestling with God and emerging from that place changed in the depths of my heart. I will never forget the physical darkness that seemed to mirror my own interior confusion, and the experience is forever linked to that physical place.

Once before Jacob had marked a physical spot as the place of encounter with God – when he set up a stone at Bethel (Genesis 28:18). Now he was himself marked with a physical reminder of a further encounter with God. His limp would be the permanent mark of what happened at the ford of Jabbok. It was here that he made preparations to meet his brother and finally face the music of a lifetime of manipulation and deceit. Would he ever change? It took a physical wrestling match and a battle of wills before he found redemption. But when the sun came up, he crossed the ford as a changed man. The water of the river and the before and after experience are akin to a baptism, signifying a crossing place, from the death of the old to something new. As with baptism, Jacob received his name, and would be the namesake of God's people – Israel.

Lord, help me to find the courage to persevere in prayer and to allow you to mould my heart and soul so that I am changed. Amen

LIZ HOARE

The burning bush: the place of encounter with compassion

Moses... led his flock beyond the wilderness and came to Horeb, the mountain of God. There the angel of the Lord appeared to him in a flame of fire out of a bush... Then the Lord said, 'I have observed the misery of my people who are in Egypt; I have heard their cry on account of their taskmasters. Indeed, I know their sufferings, and I have come down to deliver them...'

Like Jacob's encounter at the ford, this appearance of God to a human being in the Old Testament is called a theophany. Such a phenomenon is never God simply playing games. His appearing is always accompanied by words, and it is the message they contain that is all-important. Here Moses was shepherding his flock in a familiar place when he noticed something unusual: a bush that was aflame but not burned up. He paused to look more closely and, having got Moses' attention, God spoke to him. He revealed himself as the God of compassion who had heard his people's cry and was coming to deliver them.

Many people attest to having had an extraordinary experience they cannot explain. For some it leads to an encounter with the living God, as it did that day for Moses. An ordinary bush turned into an extraordinary encounter that revealed the character of God and instigated a call to action on Moses' part. Moses could not make this happen, and indeed at first he would rather it had not, for it was to make life-changing demands. We cannot engineer God's coming, but we can learn to pay attention so that we are attuned to the eternal in the present.

Today, as part of your prayers, think through the day ahead and ask the Lord to meet you in the ordinary places of work, home, journeying, meetings and rest. Learning to have eyes to see and ears to hear will mean also having hearts that are open to being changed as a result of seeing and hearing and responding in obedience.

Lord, may I meet you in the ordinary places and respond to your call today.
Amen

LIZ HOARE

The wilderness: the place of formation

He sustained him in a desert land, in a howling wilderness waste; he shielded him, cared for him, guarded him as the apple of his eye. As an eagle stirs up its nest, and hovers over its young; as it spreads its wings, takes them up, and bears them aloft on its pinions, the Lord alone guided him.

Wildernesses are generally unpromising places. As here, words like 'howling waste', or 'barren', 'wild', 'dry' and 'unproductive' come to mind. What good could possibly occur in such a place? Perhaps you are experiencing a wilderness in your life right now. It may not be physical, but your job, home life or even place of worship just feels barren and harsh. Today's reading is part of the so-called Song of Moses, a hymn of praise to the faithfulness of the Lord God followed by the recounting of Israel's failure to respond in a like manner and returning to God's compassion and mercy in the latter verses (Deuteronomy 32:1–43). We can see that the wilderness is the place where God shaped his people, and the landscape itself had an important part to play. In the wilderness the people were vulnerable; they had to learn to depend on God for safety and protection, as when he accompanied them in a pillar of cloud by day and fire by night. They had to rely on him for sustenance and received manna and water from the rock. They had to learn the difficult art of waiting while Moses was on the mountain with God and they experienced the stripping away of all the former things that had made their lives tolerable in Egypt. Over and over again they failed, but God remained faithful.

Today's reading offers two beautiful images of God's ways with us: we are the apple of his eye, precious beyond telling, and he watches over us like a mother eagle guarding her young. The eagle's purpose is to see her young fly and become mature eagles themselves, just as God's ways with us are forming us into the likeness of Christ, even in our wilderness places.

Lord Jesus, sustain me in my wilderness places and watch over me. Amen

LIZ HOARE

The Jordan River: the place of remembering

'Pass on before the ark of the Lord your God into the middle of the Jordan, and each of you take up a stone on his shoulder, one for each of the tribes of the Israelites, so that this may be a sign among you. When your children ask in time to come, "What do these stones mean to you?" then you shall tell them that the waters of the Jordan were cut off in front of the ark of the covenant of the Lord… So these stones shall be to the Israelites a memorial for ever.'

Places bring back memories, and collective memories are often preserved by erecting a memorial of some kind. Many standing stones are so ancient that we do not know why they are there, but they seem to represent the significance of their resting place for the people who erected them. Later, early Christians of the British Isles put up great stone crosses inscribed with images from the Christian story. They made a statement about the victory of Christ on the cross, proclaiming that Jesus was Lord. I like to imagine people telling the stories recorded on the crosses and bearing witness to the good news of the gospel. These stones in the landscape 'spoke' powerfully of God's presence and character to all who saw them, but moreover they were a prompt to believers to pass on the message to others. God had acted as he had promised and sent a saviour.

Today's passage shows that same saving God at work to lead his people into the promised land. Having crossed the river, Joshua erected the twelve stones that the representative from each tribe had carried over as a memorial to what took place there. God had warned his people of the danger of forgetting his mighty acts of protection, provision and continuing presence once they had entered their new land (Deuteronomy 8). The stones were a reminder both of his strength and of the importance of remembering.

Thank you, Lord, for the memory stones in the story of your people. May they give hope to those in places where the future looks bleak today. Amen

LIZ HOARE

Elijah on Horeb:
the place of recommissioning

[God] said, 'Go out and stand on the mountain before the Lord, for the Lord is about to pass by.' Now there was a great wind… but the Lord was not in the wind; and after the wind an earthquake, but the Lord was not in the earthquake; and after the earthquake a fire, but the Lord was not in the fire; and after the fire, a sound of sheer silence… Then there came a voice to him that said, 'What are you doing here, Elijah?'

Elijah went back the way he came, but not before he hit the depths of despair. Immediately after his great triumph on Mt Carmel and in terror of Queen Jezebel, he experienced a rollercoaster of emotions, from the heights to the depths. Having wished to die, he was sustained by the angel of the Lord in a practical way and came to a place where others before him had met with God. The place was deeply significant, but upon arriving there Elijah crept into a cave and went to sleep (v. 9). He was not yet ready to hear the Lord God speak to him. Like Moses, he witnessed natural phenomena that startled and amazed him. It was the 'sound of sheer silence' that finally summoned him to the entrance of his cave of abandonment to hear the restorative words of his Lord and master. Cowering under his mantle, he faced God's repeated question, and each time Elijah poured forth a catalogue of woe and abandonment. Then God reassured him that he was not alone and there were others to support him. It was with this reassurance that the Lord sent him back the way he had come to complete what he had begun.

Perhaps we have felt some of the emotions that Elijah experienced in his ministry: exhaustion, abandonment, failure, depression and despair. With such feelings, the future looks bleak and it's hard to find strength to go on. The place of recommissioning can be anywhere, but we too may have to allow the storm to rage within and without before we can let go and embrace God's ever-flowing compassion.

Lord, help me to listen to that still small voice today. Amen

LIZ HOARE

Isaiah in the temple: the place of healing

In the year that King Uzziah died, I saw the Lord sitting on a throne, high and lofty; and the hem of his robe filled the temple. Seraphs were in attendance above him… And one called to another and said: 'Holy, holy, holy is the Lord of hosts; the whole earth is full of his glory.'… And I said: 'Woe is me! I am lost, for I am a man of unclean lips… yet my eyes have seen the King, the Lord of hosts!' Then one of the seraphs flew to me, holding a live coal that had been taken from the altar with a pair of tongs. The seraph touched my mouth with it and said: 'Now that this has touched your lips, your guilt has departed and your sin is blotted out.' Then I heard the voice of the Lord saying, 'Whom shall I send, and who will go for us?' And I said, 'Here am I; send me!'

The power of Isaiah's vision is almost palpable. God's holiness over-whelms him, and he is stricken by his unworthiness. The vision in the temple could have been the place of destruction for him, for no one can see God and live (Exodus 33:20). Instead it became the place of healing. Fire in the Old Testament denotes the presence of the holy God. Taken directly from the altar, the holiest place, the coal's searing glow burns Isaiah's lips. God's holiness 'infects' Isaiah so that his sin is blotted out. 'Salvation' is a word that includes forgiveness of sins but also complete wholeness. It is all-encompassing: all the wounds, defects and deficiencies that we experience in this life are mended so that we become whole again.

Isaiah experienced God's amazing grace: 'I once was lost, but now am found, was blind, but now I see' (John Newton, 'Amazing Grace'). His restored condition made him ready and prepared to respond to God's call to go, whatever that might entail. God saves us not so that we may escape this world, but so that we may live the lives God intended for us here and now.

Lord, help me to enter more fully into your healing power today. Amen

LIZ HOARE

Nazareth: the place of obscurity

When they had finished everything required by the law of the Lord, they returned to Galilee, to their own town of Nazareth. The child grew and became strong, filled with wisdom; and the favour of God was upon him.

If we were planning the salvation of the world, most of us would choose auspicious beginnings, providing every resource known to humanity. God, however, persists in making unlikely choices, none more so than the circumstances of the incarnation. An occupied nation, a young girl with no prospects, a birth in squalor and, here in today's reading, an obscure town for the upbringing of his beloved son. Jesus spent the longest part of his life in Nazareth, and we are not even told what he did with all those years. We make our guesses: following in his father's footsteps as a carpenter perhaps; learning the faith of his ancestors surely, for he knew the scriptures as well as anyone. But why did God arrange things like this?

Today's world seems more complex than the age in which Jesus was born. But we know that, although knowledge has increased, wisdom is a different thing. Many people would like to be wise, but do not devote their lives to acquiring wisdom, for there is so much else to do. It seems that Jesus had a different set of priorities. 'He grew and became strong' suggests not just physical prowess but also strength of character. This goes hand in hand with becoming wise, and Luke reports that Jesus was 'filled' with wisdom.

How did he achieve this? Perhaps 'achieve' gives the wrong impression, for wisdom is not acquired by striving. It grows secretly as we attend to the important things. Luke's final comment is the clue: 'the favour of God was upon him'. He spent time with his heavenly Father, so much so that later he told people that he never did anything on his own, but only what he saw his Father doing (John 5:19). To be so in tune with God is to have gained wisdom of a kind that is beyond any price we could imagine.

Dear Lord, show me how to grow in wisdom. Amen

LIZ HOARE

Galilee: the place of calling

As Jesus passed along the Sea of Galilee, he saw Simon and his brother Andrew casting a net into the lake – for they were fishermen. And Jesus said to them, 'Follow me and I will make you fish for people.' And immediately they left their nets and followed him. As he went a little farther, he saw James son of Zebedee and his brother John, who were in their boat mending the nets. Immediately he called them; and they left their father Zebedee in the boat with the hired men, and followed him.

You may be one of those people who can recall exactly when and where you first responded to the gospel and became a follower of Jesus. Lent is a good time to pause to remember that first call: what it meant then and what it has meant since. It may have involved leaving behind a whole way of life, even family and friends, in order to follow where Jesus was calling you. For all of us, including those whose lives have evolved from a gradual seed of faith planted long ago, reminding ourselves of our call to follow and what it means is important.

We are called to be those who fish for people. That may involve direct evangelism. It will certainly mean that we travel through life as ambassadors for Christ, his call embedded in our DNA. Becoming a follower of Jesus will mean laying down certain things: ambitions, relationships, lifestyles and anything that threatens to encumber us in serving our new master. We are learning to march to a different drum. Simon, Andrew, James and John retained certain things from their old lives too: their names, the skills they had learned as fishermen (now put to new use) and their humanity.

Being called to follow Jesus involves finding out our true worth and purpose as human beings. At one point, Simon and some of the others returned to fishing for a short while, but it did not last. Their vision renewed, they set out again to follow in the footsteps of their master and Lord.

Lord, help me to love myself with open eyes,
so that I may more truly love you. Amen

LIZ HOARE

The well at Sychar: the place of insight

But [Jesus] had to go through Samaria. So he came to a Samaritan city called Sychar, near the plot of ground that Jacob had given to his son Joseph. Jacob's well was there, and Jesus, tired out by his journey, was sitting by the well. It was about noon. A Samaritan woman came to draw water, and Jesus said to her, 'Give me a drink.'

Did Jesus know that a disreputable woman would arrive with her water jar as he sat in the heat and dust of noonday? The story unfolds with a conversation that includes humour, challenge, question and answer, red herrings and more. The well at Sychar was a good place to gather for some conversation, especially for the women of the village drawing water for their daily needs, but Jesus was not there just for the idle chatter. He turned a simple request into a dialogue that was about life in all its fullness.

Later in his gospel, John describes Jesus crying out, 'Let anyone who is thirsty come to me, and let the one who believes in me drink. As the scripture has said, "Out of the believer's heart shall flow rivers of living water"' (John 7:37–38). It is a commentary on what happened as the woman moved from defensiveness about her past to curiosity about Jesus and then to realising that she was speaking to someone who could fulfil her deepest longings.

What is it that we long for? Sometimes the business of keeping up appearances or even just keeping going obscures our deepest needs so that we are unable to see what God is offering us. We think we have to do something dramatic to find release, or peace, or whatever it is we desire, but it is here in the midst of it all, if we could but see. The woman stayed at the well because she was intrigued and then captivated by Jesus. She had the privilege of his sitting in front of her. We too may come close and hear him speaking into our lives, so that we gain the insight needed to quench our thirst with the water of life.

Lord Jesus, give me to drink from the well of salvation today. Amen

LIZ HOARE

The mountain: the place of transfiguration

Six days later, Jesus took with him Peter and James and John, and led them up a high mountain apart, by themselves. And he was transfigured before them, and his clothes became dazzling white, such as no one on earth could bleach them. And there appeared to them Elijah with Moses, who were talking with Jesus. Then Peter said to Jesus, 'Rabbi, it is good for us to be here; let us make three dwellings, one for you, one for Moses, and one for Elijah.' He did not know what to say, for they were terrified. Then a cloud overshadowed them, and from the cloud there came a voice, 'This is my Son, the Beloved; listen to him!'

In this extraordinary event, Peter, James and John saw and heard things far beyond their human experience to date. It is no wonder they were terrified! Peter is often castigated for his exclamation, but he may have been more aware than we think of what was taking place and have wanted simply to honour the divinity that was present. Whatever he thought at the time, he came to realise that he had been with God on the mountain and had witnessed a whole other reality. He saw something of God's glory. God's glory was revealed and for a moment the disciples were caught up into God's eternity. This was to have a lasting effect on Peter and how he understood Jesus (cf. 2 Peter 1:16–18). It is a reminder that in Christ, heaven has come close and there is so much more to be revealed.

Every place has the potential to be the place where God's glory may be glimpsed in ways that transfigure the situation and enable us to see it from God's eternal perspective. Above all, we are challenged, like the disciples, to listen to God's son, Jesus, and obey. The Latin word for 'obey' contains the meaning 'to listen'. The two actions are closely linked. God's transfiguring presence invites us to be part of the change that is needed.

Lord, help me to listen to Jesus, the Lord of glory,
and learn to see things from your perspective. Amen

LIZ HOARE

The home of Mary, Martha and Lazarus: the place of friendship

Now a certain man was ill, Lazarus of Bethany, the village of Mary and her sister Martha. Mary was the one who anointed the Lord with perfume and wiped his feet with her hair; her brother Lazarus was ill. So the sisters sent a message to Jesus, 'Lord, he whom you love is ill.'

These few verses tell us a great deal about the home at Bethany and Jesus' relationship with it and its occupants. Bethany was a small village outside Jerusalem frequented by Jesus, who found refuge and friendship there. Mary, Martha and Lazarus seem to have been as family to him, and perhaps it was one of the few places where he could relax and enjoy company over food and conversation. It is a reminder of the human side of Jesus, a reminder that the incarnation involved the Word's becoming flesh and blood. If we downplay this, we risk inventing a Jesus who cannot share our humanity at any level.

As today's reading unfolds, we witness the humanity of Jesus in vivid detail as he weeps over the death of his dear friend. 'Surely he has borne our griefs' (Isaiah 53:4, ESV)? But the home at Bethany is a place where Jesus' divinity is touched on also. Key events took place there and John reminds us of one of them: the anointing of Jesus' feet by Mary shortly before his crucifixion (see John 12:1–8). This was a prophetic act on her part, which Jesus regarded as preparation for his death. Mary's costly and extravagant gesture was one of deep love, poured out for him as he would pour out his life for her and for all of us in his death.

Clearly this little family loved Jesus, and their mutual vulnerability had built trust and a depth of friendship that was Mary and Martha's strongest hope in a time of crisis. At this stage Jesus was their brother's only hope. Jesus did not need their bold reminder that Lazarus was beloved, but then as now he delights to hear our words of love and devotion.

Lord Jesus, thank you that you call us friends.
Help me to grow in friendship with you. Amen

LIZ HOARE

Gethsemane: the place of struggle

They went to a place called Gethsemane; and [Jesus] said to his disciples, 'Sit here while I pray.' He took with him Peter and James and John, and began to be distressed and agitated. And he said to them, 'I am deeply grieved, even to death; remain here, and keep awake.' And going a little farther, he threw himself on the ground and prayed that, if it were possible, the hour might pass from him. He said, 'Abba, Father, for you all things are possible; remove this cup from me; yet, not what I want, but what you want.'

Gethsemane was a favourite location of Jesus, who often met there with his disciples (see John 18:2). It was a garden of olive trees on the slope of the Mount of Olives, and the name literally means 'olive press.' All four gospels describe events there just before Jesus' crucifixion, and it was a place of enormous significance for Jesus. Jesus knew that the great crisis of his earthly life was approaching, so he went to a place where he could pray. He also wanted company in his hour of need, so he took with him his closest disciples. He asked them to keep vigil, but the struggle was his alone. Wrestling in prayer, he faced the future with dread, even as he sought the presence of his heavenly Father.

We may have witnessed someone struggling with what lies ahead and seen how body, mind and spirit are all caught up in agony. Jesus was 'distressed' and 'agitated' and the word he used of himself was 'grieved'. These are all characteristics of someone undergoing a great struggle. Does it shock us that Jesus shrank from his ordeal and sought release 'if possible'? The scene records a battle of cosmic proportions going on and Jesus at the heart of it. Yet to the end he desired to align his will with the Father. In our own struggles, it is not a cop-out to echo Jesus' prayer, for prayer is above all about aligning our wills with the will of the Lord of the universe, who works all things together for good.

Not my will but yours be done, dear Lord. Amen

LIZ HOARE

Calvary: the place of remembrance

One of the criminals who were hanged there kept deriding him and saying, 'Are you not the Messiah? Save yourself and us.' But the other rebuked him, saying, 'Do you not fear God…?' Then he said, 'Jesus, remember me when you come into your kingdom.' He replied, 'Truly I tell you, today you will be with me in Paradise.' It was now about noon, and darkness came over the whole land until three in the afternoon, while the sun's light failed; and the curtain of the temple was torn in two. Then Jesus, crying with a loud voice, said, 'Father, into your hands I commend my spirit.' Having said this, he breathed his last.

The fear of being forgotten is a deeply held human trait and one of the main reasons why death is so threatening. Who will remember us when we're gone? The second criminal had it right when he asked Jesus to remember him. The irony of the first criminal's words is striking when placed alongside Jesus' response to the plea of the second. Jesus was indeed the Messiah, but his kingdom is not of this world, though it is being established even now in this world and one day will be complete. Believers inhabit both realms, and salvation crosses the divide. The two sayings from the cross recorded here show Jesus first of all reassuring the second criminal that he would remember him, while his words to his heavenly Father show the trust he had that God would not abandon or forget his beloved son. Placed alongside his words in John, 'It is finished' (John 19:30), Jesus' act of relinquishment of his life and breath is done with confidence that God will remember his commitment to him and receive him in glory.

We can pray this prayer in trust each day as we lie down to sleep, and it holds true for us as we draw our final breath also. God is faithful, and he will remember us. After all, he knows us by name, we are his, because of the battle that Jesus won on the cross.

Jesus, remember me when you come into your kingdom. Amen

LIZ HOARE

Exile

In recent years we have become all too familiar with tragic tales of exile. From the safety of our homes, we have witnessed on our screens the plight of those who, forced to flee their homeland because of poverty or violence, find themselves crushed into fragile boats as they make desperate journeys to new lands. These lands will inevitably be for them places of exile. Some of them may be acquainted with the biblical stories of the exile. Lamentations, several of the psalms and the cries of the exilic prophets will resonate deeply with their experience, offering comfort in the companionship of those ancient people who not only survived in exile but also found the precious gift of hope.

But this expulsion from a beloved homeland is not the only form of exile. Exile is where you find yourself feeling not at home: the place that seems unfamiliar, where you are deprived of those home comforts that normally make you feel safe in this world. The moment we are born we experience exile, as we are evicted from the safe haven of the womb. From that moment on we can experience all kinds of exiles as we journey through life: starting a new school, moving to a new town, losing the safety and familiarity of a significant friendship, working in an environment that feels hostile, living in a world that feels alien because of illness or injury, and many others. Though many of these may not have the terrible severity of being uprooted from your homeland, nevertheless they can feel hugely disturbing. Lent can be a form of voluntary exile – where we choose to deprive ourselves of something that would normally be one of the comforts of home.

As we explore the scriptures, we see many stories of humans like ourselves who found themselves in an exile situation and who looked to God for help. And what we find is that exile can be full of possibility and wonder. It can also be a place of discovering the presence of God in surprising ways. In the next two weeks we shall look at some of these stories and draw inspiration from them for the times when life takes us into experiences of exile.

MICHAEL MITTON

Exile from Eden

Then the Lord God said, 'See, the man has become like one of us, knowing good and evil; and now, he might reach out his hand and take also from the tree of life, and eat, and live for ever' – therefore the Lord God sent him forth from the garden of Eden, to till the ground from which he was taken. He drove out the man; and at the east of the garden of Eden he placed the cherubim, and a sword flaming and turning to guard the way to the tree of life.

The first two chapters of the Bible describe a place and tell a story. The place is a garden that is the most special of all gardens. It is a place unspoilt by any kind of damage. The story is about the creation of two human beings who inhabit this beautiful place perfectly. They are in harmony with each other and with God. Nothing tarnishes this wonderful world, until we get to chapter 3, and then it feels as if all hell breaks loose, and in many senses it does. It is almost unbearable to read of the terrible decisions the humans take as they imagine that there is even greener grass on the other side of this perfect world. As a consequence of their decision, they are exiled from this garden, and the rest of the Bible is about humans trying to find their way back.

It is good to return to this story from time to time, not to analyse it but to dwell in it – to read the first chapters and connect with our own longing for this unspoilt paradise, and then to feel the sense of loss as we depart with Adam and Eve to the land beyond that flaming sword. We realise it is not their story, but our story. However comfortable or safe we may feel in this world, there is always that nagging doubt that things could be better. Lent is an excellent time for listening to this yearning. Such a yearning properly disturbs our settledness and stirs us to pray 'your kingdom come… on earth as it is in heaven' (Matthew 6:10) – and to work for it.

Lord, may your kingdom come in this world, as it is in paradise.

MICHAEL MITTON

Lament in exile

How lonely sits the city that once was full of people! How like a widow she has become, she that was great among the nations! She that was a princess among the provinces has become a vassal. She weeps bitterly in the night, with tears on her cheeks; among all her lovers she has no one to comfort her; all her friends have dealt treacherously with her, they have become her enemies. Judah has gone into exile with suffering and hard servitude…

The destruction of Jerusalem by Nebuchadnezzar in 587BC, and the enforced exile in Babylon of many of its citizens, was a horrendous calamity for the people of God. The impossible had happened, and the result was death, starvation, destruction and exile. Those traumatised people who found themselves as captives in a foreign land needed words to give expression to the overwhelming sense of devastation and loss they had experienced. The book of Lamentations is an attempt to provide such words.

If you are well and content, the words of this book will probably just seem depressing. However, if you find yourself in any kind of exile, this book is a remarkable gift. It is written by one who has managed to find words to express their emotional jumble of grief, failure, guilt, fear and rage. They say it as it is. What is wonderful is that they feel they can do this safely in the presence of God, because they have discovered that God is one who listens compassionately to human suffering. Yes, in their case, their exile was partly of their own making, and there is penitence in these lamentations. But more than anything, this book gives permission to any of us to express our hurt and suffering to God, and to know that such laments are held in the heart of heaven.

And set right in the middle of the book is an astonishing cry of hope, because lamenting in the presence of God opens our hearts to perceiving his compassion and love: 'But this I call to mind, and therefore I have hope: The steadfast love of the Lord never ceases, his mercies never come to an end' (Lamentations 3:21–22).

Compassionate God, thank you for hearing my laments.

MICHAEL MITTON

Memory in exile

Listen to me, you that pursue righteousness, you that seek the Lord. Look to the rock from which you were hewn, and to the quarry from which you were dug. Look to Abraham your father and to Sarah who bore you; for he was but one when I called him, but I blessed him and made him many. For the Lord will comfort Zion; he will comfort all her waste places, and will make her wilderness like Eden, her desert like the garden of the Lord…

The second part of the book of Isaiah is often called 'the book of comfort' and is addressed to exiles. It begins with the famous 'Comfort my people' exhortation in chapter 40, and it includes the references to the servant of God, who not only comforts the people but also suffers with them. In the midst of this section comes the wonderful promise that God will not only comfort broken Zion but will also transform its wilderness, that it might flourish like the garden of Eden. The passage evokes that yearning for Eden again. And how is this hope engaged? The prophet says that the path is found by the act of remembering.

Remembering is a key discipline for exiles. But it is a particular type of remembering. It is not a harking back to the good old days or a wallowing in nostalgia. It is a remembering that empowers for the future. In the case of today's passage, the exiles are invited to remember Abraham and Sarah, to recall their faith and the fact that God worked such wonders through them. If God brought such abundance of generations from a couple who were apparently past their childbearing years, then he can breathe life back into listless exiles. Such remembering kindles energising hope.

When we find ourselves in an exile situation, it is a helpful discipline to look back at the ways God has led us in the past. Lent is an excellent time for looking back and retelling for ourselves and others how God has worked in us. Such remembering can open us to new possibilities of faith.

Breathe on my memories, Holy Spirit, that my remembering
may lead me to discover the gardens of the Lord.

MICHAEL MITTON

Presence in exile

In the thirtieth year, in the fourth month, on the fifth day of the month, as I was among the exiles by the river Chebar, the heavens were opened, and I saw visions of God. On the fifth day of the month (it was the fifth year of the exile of King Jehoiachin), the word of the Lord came to the priest Ezekiel son of Buzi, in the land of the Chaldeans by the river Chebar; and the hand of the Lord was on him there.

One of the people uprooted from Jerusalem and hauled into exile was a young priest called Ezekiel. The traditional belief was that God gave his people a specific land – the land of Israel – and at the centre of this land was the great city of Zion, which was the city of God. And the place where God dwelt most directly was in the temple built by the great King Solomon. Knock down the temple and destroy the city and utter chaos would ensue, for where would God abide? The people of Israel who were marched into captivity in Babylon were faced not only with a terrible social crisis but a theological one as well. As they saw it, God had effectively been evicted from his land. How could they possibly ever make contact with him again?

Well, it seems that Ezekiel was open to a development of this theology. Perhaps it surprised him as much as anyone else that while he was dwelling in the very place of desolation he saw visions of God. Jerusalem was closed for business, but heaven was open. From that moment Ezekiel became a remarkable seer, witnessing visions that have intrigued, baffled and delighted people ever since. These visions proved one thing clearly – God was not confining his presence to just one place and one temple. His presence was available even in exile.

Exile brings disturbance. We may feel deprived of the usual routines that help us connect with God. Ezekiel would tell us that this is the ideal setting for gaining new visions of God. Any place can be the starting point for gaining a new vision of God.

Lord God, give me the eyes to behold visions of you.

MICHAEL MITTON

Hope in exile

Then he said to me, 'Prophesy to the breath, prophesy, mortal, and say to the breath: Thus says the Lord God: Come from the four winds, O breath, and breathe upon these slain, that they may live.' I prophesied as he commanded me, and the breath came into them, and they lived, and stood on their feet, a vast multitude. Then he said to me, 'Mortal, these bones are the whole house of Israel. They say, "Our bones are dried up, and our hope is lost; we are cut off completely."'

We stay with Ezekiel for another day. He is a prophet specifically called by God to work with people in exile. His task is to lift them from a rather parochial view of God to something much bigger. There is much in the first part of his book that is about judgement on the people of God for their infidelity, and those listening to this prophet would be in no doubt that they had been the cause of their own downfall. Then from chapter 33 we start hearing messages of hope. The people have to acknowledge the bad news before they can fully appreciate the good news.

The message of hope is none other than the message of resurrection. The vision of the valley of dry bones is effectively saying that the exiles don't amount to anything more than a pile of dead bones. All hope is lost. However, there is one thing that can change all of this – the breath of God. The God of the impossible can transform the bones of death into an army of life. The breath of God creates a new future. And how does the breath come? It is summoned by the prophet.

Another discipline of exile is the inbreathing of new life. In Christ, we too can engage prophetically in the great act of invoking the Holy Spirit of God to quicken that which has apparently died. Ezekiel would encourage us to recognise that the moment when our normal securities are removed may be the very time to summon the breath of God. Even in Lent we are a resurrection people.

If you are aware of an apparently lifeless situation today,
call on the breath of God for new life.

MICHAEL MITTON

Love in exile

So [Naomi] said, 'See, your sister-in-law has gone back to her people and to her gods; return after your sister-in-law.' But Ruth said, 'Do not press me to leave you or to turn back from following you! Where you go, I will go; where you lodge, I will lodge; your people shall be my people, and your God my God. Where you die, I will die – there will I be buried.'

One of the most tragic stories of exile comes in the book of Ruth. It begins with Naomi. She, her husband and sons are forced into exile because of famine. They flee to Moab, a one-time enemy of Israel's. There the two sons marry Moabite women, but Naomi's husband and two sons die. A more tragic scene is hard to imagine. Naomi decides she must return to her homeland. Her daughter-in-law, Ruth, decides to opt for voluntary exile because of the great love she has developed for Naomi. Today's reading is a remarkable declaration of love and commitment to someone not only of a different nationality, but from a nation that has been an enemy.

Thus Ruth and Naomi make their way to Bethlehem. Ruth is now a widow in exile and is very vulnerable. Naomi is back home, and yet her severely bereaved soul is still in exile; she exclaims, 'the Almighty has dealt bitterly with me' (v. 20). Ruth, however, seems to harbour no bitterness, and in time she meets Boaz, who takes her as his bride. The story ends with Naomi cradling her grandson and a new hope-filled future opens for her.

Both Ruth and Naomi have to suffer the literal exile of dwelling in a foreign land, and the emotional exile of bereavement, where those who gave them safety are taken from them. It is Ruth the foreigner who excels in this story. She chooses the way of love even in the vulnerability of exile. And it is in exile that she experiences being the beloved. In exile we can throw up our hands and complain that God has treated us bitterly. Or, like Ruth, we can choose the way of love.

Lord, in my exile help me choose the way of love.

MICHAEL MITTON

45

Heaven's exiles

Peter, an apostle of Jesus Christ. To the exiles of the Dispersion in Pontus, Galatia, Cappadocia, Asia, and Bithynia, who have been chosen and destined by God the Father and sanctified by the Spirit to be obedient to Jesus Christ and to be sprinkled with his blood: May grace and peace be yours in abundance. Blessed be the God and Father of our Lord Jesus Christ! By his great mercy he has given us a new birth into a living hope through the resurrection of Jesus Christ from the dead.

In this passage, and in 1 Peter 2:11, words are used that are translated in many English versions as 'exile'. Peter clearly held to a view that for those who follow Christ there is something about our existence here on earth that makes us not quite at home in this world. The followers of Jesus carry a destiny that is to do with heaven; they are people who have been spiritually birthed into a new identity due to the resurrection of Jesus. The words Peter employs were often used of someone who lived in a strange land and who carried a homesickness, such that their thoughts often turned to, and their first loyalty was to, that home. It is that yearning for Eden that we met in our earlier reading.

This image of exile describes our relationship with this world to which God has sent us. Jesus often taught about the kingdom of heaven, which is the true place of belonging for his followers. If this is the case, how should we live in this world? If we take the Babylonian exile as an example, then it means we put down roots in this world and learn ways of flourishing as exiles. But we will always hold to the values of the kingdom and this will often throw us into conflict with this world, a conflict that in the end led Jesus to the cross. But the resurrection revealed the true nature of the kingdom of heaven. Exiles can be a wonderful gift to a nation, and the call of heaven's exiles is to bring heaven's resurrection gifts to the land where we dwell.

Lord, make me a blessing to the land where I dwell.

MICHAEL MITTON

Empowered in exile

In those days Jesus came from Nazareth of Galilee and was baptised by John in the Jordan. And just as he was coming up out of the water, he saw the heavens torn apart and the Spirit descending like a dove on him. And a voice came from heaven, 'You are my Son, the Beloved; with you I am well pleased.' And the Spirit immediately drove him out into the wilderness. He was in the wilderness for forty days, tempted by Satan; and he was with the wild beasts; and the angels waited on him.

This passage is how Mark introduces his readers to the person of Jesus. The Son of God's arrival in this world is heralded by the prophet John, who greets him in the waters of the Jordan and plunges him under that flowing river in the ritual of baptism. As Jesus is immersed in the waters of this earth, so heaven opens and out comes none other than the Holy Spirit of God. Surprisingly, the Spirit appears not in an image of mighty power, but in the meek form of a dove – very much like our common wood pigeon. Perhaps one of the reasons that the third person of the Trinity should take such a humble form is that the rock dove is a natural inhabitant of the desert, and it is into that habitat that the Spirit leads Jesus. For Jesus, who is fully human, this environment is a place of exile – it is far from comfortable.

It is a truly fascinating start to the gospel and, among other things, it tells us that the Holy Spirit may well lead any of us into places that feel to us exilic, yet to the Spirit are home. Jesus leads the way for us and shows that, though the place of exile can be tough and there are battles to be had there, it can also be a place of renewal and overcoming. If we allow the Spirit to lead us, we may feel surprisingly at home there.

Holy Spirit, grant me an open heart to follow your pathways.

MICHAEL MITTON

Faith in exile

When [Jesus] entered Capernaum, a centurion came to him, appealing to him and saying, 'Lord, my servant is lying at home paralysed, in terrible distress.' And he said to him, 'I will come and cure him.' The centurion answered, 'Lord, I am not worthy to have you come under my roof; but only speak the word, and my servant will be healed… When Jesus heard him, he was amazed and said to those who followed him, 'Truly I tell you, in no one in Israel have I found such faith.'

Though the people of God returned to the land of Israel after the Babylonian exile, they never felt the land was truly theirs, as it was occupied by a succession of foreign powers. In fact, they still spoke of this experience as exile – they could not be truly at home in their homeland. At the time of Jesus, those responsible for this 'exile' were the Romans and they were regarded as oppressors who tainted the precious holy land with their Gentile presence.

Today's story involves one such Roman – a senior soldier who, much to everyone's surprise, comes to Jesus for help. Those watching would have eagerly expected Jesus to take full opportunity in this encounter for proclaiming fearful judgements on this defiant pagan who was polluting the land. Instead, Jesus does quite the opposite. He not only heals the servant of the centurion, but he then commends this Gentile oppressor for having more faith about him than the most pious of the religious establishment. This would not have gone down well with that establishment!

But Jesus noticed the activity of the Spirit in that centurion's heart. The Spirit was at work in the desert. The Romans may have been the perpetrators of exile, but even that did not put them out of reach of God's grace. For Jesus, exile was not about land and power. Anyone who lacked faith was in exile. The one growing in faith was on the journey home.

At any point in life we can feel oppressed by others. But there may be times when the oppressor experiences a raw human need, as did that centurion. Such moments can create openings for extraordinary faith.

Lord, keep my eyes always open to signs of faith in unexpected places.

MICHAEL MITTON

Revelation in exile

Now when Jesus came into the district of Caesarea Philippi, he asked his disciples, 'Who do people say that the Son of Man is?'... Simon Peter answered, 'You are the Messiah, the Son of the living God.' And Jesus answered him, 'Blessed are you, Simon son of Jonah! For flesh and blood has not revealed this to you, but my Father in heaven. And I tell you, you are Peter, and on this rock I will build my church, and the gates of Hades will not prevail against it.'

In today's story, Jesus has taken his disciples on a long journey north to the city of Caesarea Philippi. This was an area full of ancient temples dedicated to the worship of Baal, and it was also the centre of Pan worship. Herod also built there a huge temple for the worship of Caesar. It is a rocky place and visitors today can still see the opening to the great chasm that was believed to be the gateway to Hades. The disciples were no doubt disturbed that Jesus should lead them to such an unholy place.

And yet here in this very place, which would have felt very much like an exile place to the disciples, Jesus, in the affirmation of Peter, reveals himself to be the Messiah, the Son of God. And not only this, but here he plants his church, using the analogy of the great rocks of the place, even referring to the gates of Hades.

This story is full of symbolism and meaning, but perhaps one of the messages that Jesus was conveying to his disciples was his desire that his church was to be present and active in the very places that upright, religious people chose to avoid. In such places Jesus wished to reveal his glory through the witness of the church. Here he would see to it that the gates that imprisoned so many people would give way to the power of the gospel.

It is all too easy to write some places off as ungodly, and yet these may be the very places where Jesus wishes to make his presence felt. And he does this through you and me – his church.

Lord Jesus, let your glory shine through me today.

MICHAEL MITTON

Praise in exile

After they had given them a severe flogging, they threw them into prison and ordered the jailer to keep them securely. Following these instructions, he put them in the innermost cell and fastened their feet in the stocks. About midnight Paul and Silas were praying and singing hymns to God, and the prisoners were listening to them. Suddenly there was an earthquake, so violent that the foundations of the prison were shaken; and immediately all the doors were opened and everyone's chains were unfastened.

Paul and Silas are on one of their great mission trips, and in this story we find them in Philippi, a mostly Gentile city in eastern Macedonia. Their stay in this city is focused around three people: Lydia, from the higher echelons of that society; a slave girl, who was regarded as barely human; and the jailer, a Roman citizen from the middle classes. Paul and Silas have clearly become at home with all strata of society.

However, there is no shortage of people who are opposed to these evangelists, and it is not long before Paul and Silas find themselves flogged and thrown into jail. The severe flogging was enough to kill some people. They survive, but have to spend the night in chains in the foul inner cell. A more hostile exile is hard to imagine. And yet, despite the pain, darkness and imprisonment, we find Paul and Silas singing at the tops of their voices as if they are at a Christian summer celebration. You wonder how they manage to 'sing the Lord's song in a foreign land' (Psalm 137:4). Clearly some work of grace has seeped so deeply into their hearts that an inner world has become more powerful than the outer world they inhabit. From the inner cells of their hearts they praise and worship God.

Some exiles can feel very hostile. But any one of us can reach into the inner cells of our own hearts and find there the presence of the one who truly sets us free. The Holy Spirit delights to lead us to such places, for where the Spirit is, there is freedom (2 Corinthians 3:17).

Lord, when I feel imprisoned, let me follow the trail of your Spirit to find true freedom.

MICHAEL MITTON

The body in exile

For while we are still in this tent, we groan under our burden, because we wish not to be unclothed but to be further clothed, so that what is mortal may be swallowed up by life. He who has prepared us for this very thing is God, who has given us the Spirit as a guarantee. So we are always confident; even though we know that while we are at home in the body we are away from the Lord – for we walk by faith, not by sight.

Today's passage is part of a complex piece of Paul's correspondence with the Christians in Corinth. One of the questions that arose in that infant church was quite what to do with the body, with all its lusts and appetites. It seems there were some who thought that following Christ gave licence to give in to these appetites (1 Corinthians 6:12–20). There were almost certainly others who would have been influenced by those Greek and Roman philosophers who saw the soul as a higher creature weighed down by the rebellious body. It was not just the first-century Christians who struggled with this – the human body has troubled the church in every generation since. Quite what do we do with it when it lets us down?

In 1 Corinthians 15 Paul introduces the notion of the resurrection body. If you take this into account, today's passage seems to suggest that we need to regard our present bodies as temporary in the grand scheme of things. If we settle down too much in this body, we run the risk of being so focused on it that we drift away from the Lord. On the other hand, these bodies will one day in Christ be transformed into something truly glorious, and for that reason they should be honoured and appreciated. In one respect dwelling in this mortal body is a sign of our exile. As we have seen, it is possible to flourish in exile, but we never cease our yearning for our true home. The vision of our future home can transform our present exile.

Lord, let me be a good steward of the body you have entrusted to me for my sojourn in this world.

MICHAEL MITTON

God in exile

Do nothing from selfish ambition or conceit, but in humility regard others as better than yourselves... Let the same mind be in you that was in Christ Jesus, who, though he was in the form of God, did not regard equality with God as something to be exploited, but emptied himself, taking the form of a slave, being born in human likeness. And being found in human form, he humbled himself and became obedient to the point of death – even death on a cross.

In some churches, at a Communion service the congregation says the words of the Nicene Creed, which includes these words about Jesus: 'For us and for our salvation he came down from heaven, was incarnate from the Holy Spirit and was made man.' It goes on to say that 'he ascended into heaven'. The early writers of our creed would have been influenced by such passages as today's reading from Philippians. This is a well-known passage that describes the humbling of Jesus, who descended from the glorious habitation of heaven to this broken world, and who lived and died among us before returning to his natural homeland. In other words, while he was with us in his incarnated form, he was living in exile.

As we think about his life as an exile, we see that Jesus most certainly flourished in this world. Though he 'emptied himself', he lived life to the full. He did not behave as a visitor – he made himself at home. He was born into the world and spent time growing up from an infant into a teenager and adult. He put down roots and made friends. He learned the language of the people. But he also kept talking about his homeland, and demonstrating what it was like. He spoke about it in such a way that something lit up in the hearts of the people, so much so that they started to long to visit his homeland. In time he explained that he had opened the door for all who wished to follow him to be part of that home.

Jesus' time in exile cost him his life. But imagine where we would be now had he chosen to stay at home!

Dear Jesus, thank you for making yourself at home in my world.

MICHAEL MITTON

God at home

Then I saw a new heaven and a new earth; for the first heaven and the first earth had passed away, and the sea was no more. And I saw the holy city, the new Jerusalem, coming down out of heaven from God, prepared as a bride adorned for her husband. And I heard a loud voice from the throne saying, 'See, the home of God is among mortals. He will dwell with them; they will be his peoples, and God himself will be with them.'

The writer of the book of Revelation is called John, and he tells us that he is writing from the island of Patmos (Revelation 1:9), which was probably a Roman penal settlement. He is therefore an author writing in exile and, as we saw with Ezekiel, living in exile provides a fertile environment for prophetic visions. In the earlier chapters of his book he details specific prophecies for local churches, but as the book moves on he covers a much wider sweep of cosmic history. In his spirit he sees terrifying judgements on the earth that culminate in a triumphant defeat of Satan, death and Hades (Revelation 20). This leads on to a most beautiful vision of the new heaven and new earth, and we are treated to a glorious vision of a healed and reformed universe with God once again dwelling fully with his created humans. We have returned to paradise and the exile from that garden is finally over.

What is particularly wonderful and extraordinary is the cry that John hears coming from the throne of God, which declares that 'the home of God is among mortals'. However we understand this mysterious prophecy of the last times, this cry from heaven is utterly heart-warming. It tells us that the place where God feels most at home is among mortals. There is perhaps no vision more compelling than this one to declare that God is most at home when he is in the company of the humans he created. He therefore yearns for that day when he can fully dwell with us again. Until that time we are all in a season of exile, but an exile full of possibility and promise.

Even so, come, Lord Jesus.

MICHAEL MITTON

To Calvary and beyond

Starting on the Fifth Sunday of Lent, the readings for the next two weeks trace Jesus' journey to Jerusalem with his disciples and what happened there. We follow Luke's account, with references to the other gospels, while I occasionally take episodes out of their narrative sequence in order to draw out a theme or emphasis.

Luke is a superb storyteller, with vividly portrayed people and settings, and it is no surprise that – out of the four gospels – his version of events is often the most familiar. He uses contrast to make a point, pairing stories of repentance with stubbornness, humility with pride, belief with unbelief. He also highlights the favourable responses of those who, for a variety of reasons, are marginal to the society of the time – whose physical or material condition, gender or religious status place them 'at the edges'.

Time and again, it is these 'edge' people, the marginal figures, who take a step forward in understanding at least something of who Jesus is and what he is talking about. Over the next fortnight, we will meet a blind beggar, a tax collector and a Roman centurion (among others), who each respond wholeheartedly to the invitation held out to them by the Son of God. Despite (or maybe because of) who they are, they 'get it' in a way that a certain rich man, and representatives of the religious authorities, and – most depressingly – Jesus' own disciples do not 'get it'.

We can assume too easily that we would not have made the same mistake. Reading these familiar stories, we can be tempted to congratulate ourselves that we would have understood right from the start, because here we are reading *New Daylight* as present-day followers of Jesus. But a moment's reflection on life – and especially on our life as the body of Christ in our local churches – shows that we can miss the point and get things wrong as easily as Peter and the other eleven disciples. There is always more for us to learn of God and the ways of God's working in the world.

As I have prepared these readings, Henry Wansbrough's commentary on Luke (BRF, 1998) has been a particular help.

NAOMI STARKEY

The disciples don't understand

Jesus took the Twelve aside and told them, 'We are going up to Jerusalem, and everything that is written by the prophets about the Son of Man will be fulfilled. He will be handed over to the Gentiles. They will mock him, insult him and spit on him; they will flog him and kill him. On the third day he will rise again.' The disciples did not understand any of this. Its meaning was hidden from them, and they did not know what he was talking about.

Today, the Fifth Sunday of Lent, was traditionally designated 'Passion Sunday', although this designation has now generally lapsed. Worshippers had the opportunity to start reflecting on the 'passion' or suffering of Jesus before Palm Sunday began the countdown through Holy Week to Good Friday itself.

Our Bible reading is a salutary reminder that there is more to suffering than physical pain – because Jesus would surely have been grieved by his disciples' failure to understand what would happen to him. At this late stage in his ministry, he tells them in unflinching detail exactly what he will endure on their forthcoming visit to the capital city: mocked, insulted, flogged and killed at the hands of the Gentiles. But his own followers, his closest friends, 'did not know what he was talking about'.

If we are ever tempted to despair because of our fellow Christians, if we are ever overwhelmed by frustration at other people's inability to understand the good news, we can imagine, just a little, the loneliness that must have lain at the heart of Jesus' ministry. As we will read in a few days, 'the Son of Man came to seek and to save the lost' (Luke 19:10), yet even those who were part of his band of disciples continued to flounder and be lost in confusion as to what Jesus' work was actually about.

Loving Lord Jesus, friend and brother, help us when we struggle to make sense of your call and your purposes for our lives. Give us patience with those among whom we live and worship and minister, that when they fail to grasp your truth, we can walk together with them into your light.

NAOMI STARKEY

The children understand

People were also bringing babies to Jesus for him to place his hands on them. When the disciples saw this, they rebuked them. But Jesus called the children to him and said, 'Let the little children come to me, and do not hinder them, for the kingdom of God belongs to such as these. Truly I tell you, anyone who will not receive the kingdom of God like a little child will never enter it.'

This is a popular Bible reading for services of infant (and child) baptism – and it may well bring to mind a happy, sunlit scene of Jesus surrounded by smiling youngsters. Such a scene is entirely possible, of course, but we should not let it beguile us away from the sharp point that the gospel writer is making here.

Luke's gospel is flavoured with a bias towards the poor, marginalised and overlooked parts of the community – a bias evident in the subversive text known as the Magnificat. Mary's song of praise (Luke 1:46–55), proclaimed while visiting her cousin Elizabeth, speaks of scattering the proud and sending 'the rich away empty'. That same note of defiance is clear in this apparently homely episode of Jesus and the children – because, says Jesus as he overrules his high-handed disciples, 'the kingdom of God belongs to such as these'.

Stop and read those words again: the kingdom of God, no less, 'belongs' to 'such as these'. Jesus does not say that there is room for the children too, that they can be squeezed in somewhere, provided they're quiet and well-behaved. He says that the kingdom belongs to them, to the children. And we should remember that children were not indulged and treasured as they are in many parts of the world today. They were weak, economically unproductive and tolerated at best or (as here) ordered out of the way. Jesus' words are breathtaking in their rebuke to his culture's norms and practices.

Loving Lord Jesus, friend and brother, we pray for the grace and humility to grasp what it means to receive your kingdom as little children. Challenge our pride and shake up our complacency so that we are changed to become truly fit for your purposes.

NAOMI STARKEY

The blind man understands

As Jesus approached Jericho, a blind man was sitting by the roadside begging... He called out, 'Jesus, Son of David, have mercy on me!'... Jesus asked him, 'What do you want me to do for you?' 'Lord, I want to see,' he replied. Jesus said to him, 'Receive your sight; your faith has healed you.' Immediately he received his sight and followed Jesus, praising God. When all the people saw it, they also praised God.

Here is another example of Luke's bias towards the poor and underprivileged: the story of a blind beggar, named as Bartimaeus in Mark's version of this episode (Mark 10:46–52). Unlike so many others, this blind man sees clearly that Jesus is no ordinary rabbi, naming him 'Son of David', an important messianic title in the other gospels.

It's striking that Jesus does not automatically rush in as saviour in the situation, even though the physical need is so evident. Instead, as he stands before this sightless man, who has been reduced to seeking favours from passers-by, Jesus asks, 'What do you want me to do for you?' The man has been shouting for 'mercy', so he needs to clarify what form he wants this mercy to take, says the Son of David.

This straight question is given a straight answer, and Jesus' response is equally direct. The beggar receives his sight 'immediately' and a moment later Jesus is on his way to Jericho again, this time with a new follower whose overflowing gratitude affects the crowd. Despite Jesus' grim predictions of death just a few verses earlier (see Sunday's comment), his ministry's popularity and success must have seemed gratifyingly unstoppable to his disciples at this point.

The formerly blind man also sees that Jesus' healing action calls for a deeper response than a mere thank you. We don't know whether he simply followed Jesus down the Jericho road for a while or whether he ended up joining the wider band of disciples. Either way, the encounter changed the direction of his life.

Imagine Jesus standing before you, asking 'What do you want me to do for you?' What would your reply be?

NAOMI STARKEY

The wealthy tax collector understands...

But Zacchaeus stood up and said to the Lord, 'Look, Lord! Here and now I give half of my possessions to the poor, and if I have cheated anybody out of anything, I will pay back four times the amount.' Jesus said to him, 'Today salvation has come to this house, because this man, too, is a son of Abraham. For the Son of Man came to seek and to save the lost.'

Jesus is now passing through Jericho, where he meets Zacchaeus in the much-loved story of the wealthy tax collector who climbs a sycamore tree so that he can see over the crowd. The old Sunday school song (with actions) that tells of this 'very little man' makes it all sound rather sweet as Jesus invites himself round 'for tea', as if he was making a play date with a friendless child.

In fact, Zacchaeus would have been a deeply unpopular local figure because he was in effect a collaborator with the Roman occupiers. It wasn't a matter of working for the equivalent of a governmental tax department; he was siding with the enemy of his own people – and lining his pockets at the same time. The onlooking crowd, who a few verses back had been praising God at the healing of the blind man, now begin to mutter against Jesus for mixing with this social outcast (v. 7).

Jesus, however, offers Zacchaeus robust affirmation. Not only does he demand and receive an invitation to his home, but he affirms him as a 'son of Abraham' – an explicit reminder to the crowd that the ways of the kingdom are ways of radical hospitality, radical belonging, extending to those whom we would very much prefer to avoid. Notice, though, that this affirmation comes after the tax collector's public self-humbling. Zacchaeus basically admits that he has been a cheat but promises to pay back fourfold, which went beyond what the law demanded. Further to this, and without even being asked by Jesus, he promises to halve his personal wealth to benefit the poor.

Like the crowd, we slip into expecting God to work on our terms,
following our agenda. Let's pray to remain always open to the
full extent of God's mind-boggling grace and generosity.

NAOMI STARKEY

... but the wealthy ruler doesn't

[Jesus] said to [the ruler], 'You still lack one thing. Sell everything you have and give to the poor, and you will have treasure in heaven. Then come, follow me.' When he heard this, he became very sad, because he was very wealthy. Jesus looked at him and said, 'How hard it is for the rich to enter the kingdom of God! Indeed, it is easier for a camel to go through the eye of a needle than for someone who is rich to enter the kingdom of God.' Those who heard this asked, 'Who then can be saved?' Jesus replied, 'What is impossible with man is possible with God.'

As mentioned in the introduction, another characteristic of Luke's gospel is using contrast as a teaching method. In line with that approach, we're returning to the previous chapter to find a very different story to that of Zacchaeus. While the tax collector announces a halving of his wealth as well as an astonishingly generous payback for his old cheating ways, the ruler here responds very differently to his encounter with Jesus. It's true that he faces a daunting challenge: selling up and distributing all his property to the poor. His response to this challenge is emotional, a deep sadness at the cost of following Jesus, one which (it would seem) he is not prepared to pay.

The message that Jesus draws out was as countercultural then as it is today. The Hebrew scriptures taught that prosperity was a sign of God's blessing. How did that relate to wealthy people's being as good as barred from God's kingdom? The vivid image of a camel struggling to get through the eye of a needle (whether a metaphorical needle or a real, and narrow, gateway) was to underline the impossibility of the challenge, not to suggest that there might be a way round it.

We may hear this story and worry that God is making some impossible-sounding demand of us, something that feels just too costly. We should remember that God is our loving Father in heaven who gives good gifts to those who ask him (Matthew 7:11).

Father, help me to trust – and not fear – your calling on my life.

NAOMI STARKEY

The religious authorities refuse to understand

One day as Jesus was teaching the people in the temple courts and proclaiming the good news, the chief priests and the teachers of the law, together with the elders, came up to him. 'Tell us by what authority you are doing these things,' they said… He replied, 'I will also ask you a question. Tell me: John's baptism – was it from heaven, or of human origin?'… They answered, 'We don't know where it was from.' Jesus said, 'Neither will I tell you by what authority I am doing these things.'

Clearly every local religious authority 'big gun' lines up here to check out the credentials of this suspiciously popular local rabbi. What's his background? Where did he train? Is he 'sound'? This wasn't just a matter of making sure that he wasn't peddling heresy. They were challenging Jesus' authority as a teacher and, fundamentally, trying to trick him into incriminating himself in some way.

Jesus is wary of their barely concealed malice and, instead of answering their question politely, he comes back with a counter-question that confounds them. He then brings the exchange to an end and goes off to carry on his ministry. What follows (vv. 9–19) is the pointed parable of the vineyard tenants who reject the owner's authority and go so far as to kill his son. After that, these same religious leaders start to plot Jesus' arrest.

Why can the very people supposedly most tuned in to the ways of God not receive his Messiah? Why don't they respond to his teaching with the crowd's edge-of-the-seat excitement? As for so many, now as then, with a vested interest in the status quo, the prospect of change is threatening for them. They would rather seek ways of ignoring or marginalising the new teaching than test their assumptions against it. As far as recognising God's Messiah, assumptions are very firmly in place – and this young man from Nazareth most certainly does not fit. That God might be in the business of surprises does not seem to have occurred to them.

Lord Jesus, open our hearts by your Spirit so that we are ready to be surprised by you.

NAOMI STARKEY

Beware future misunderstanding

Some of his disciples were remarking about how the temple was adorned with beautiful stones and with gifts dedicated to God. But Jesus said, 'As for what you see here, the time will come when not one stone will be left on another; every one of them will be thrown down.' 'Teacher,' they asked, 'when will these things happen? And what will be the sign that they are about to take place?' He replied: 'Watch out that you are not deceived. For many will come in my name, claiming, "I am he," and, "The time is near." Do not follow them.'

Imagine being on a pilgrimage to St Paul's in London or St Peter's in Rome and commenting to your group leader on the stunning architecture – and getting the response, 'Make the most of it! It's going to be demolished in a few years' time.' The disciples would have been even more shocked hearing Jesus' response to their pleasantries about the temple. The temple was not just the national place of worship but was also seen as the dwelling place of God himself. It's where Jesus himself lingered as a boy, because it was his 'Father's house' (Luke 2:49).

Following the Jewish revolt in AD66, the temple was destroyed, never to be rebuilt. And, as Jesus had warned, in the decades before that cataclysm there was a rise in messianic movements, offering false hope and misleading instruction. Given the disciples' less-than-unblemished track record of understanding Jesus' teaching, the likelihood of their being led astray would have seemed fairly high.

We find warnings about false teaching throughout the scriptures, from Old Testament fulminations against Baal worship to the warnings in Paul's letters against the 'Judaisers' in the early years of the church. People seem to have a habit of going off on their own forays of belief. While asking questions about our faith is an essential part of growing to maturity in Christ, it is often hard to agree on what should constitute the non-negotiables of belief.

How can we maintain a good balance between cultivating a flexible and informed faith and avoiding false teaching? And how widely should we range in defining what we mean by 'false'?

NAOMI STARKEY

Jerusalem doesn't understand

As [Jesus] approached Jerusalem and saw the city, he wept over it and said, 'If you, even you, had only known on this day what would bring you peace – but now it is hidden from your eyes. The days will come upon you when your enemies will build an embankment against you and encircle you and hem you in on every side. They will dash you to the ground, you and the children within your walls. They will not leave one stone on another, because you did not recognise the time of God's coming to you.'

To mark Palm Sunday, the beginning of Holy Week, we step back in the flow of the gospel story to an emotional scene that takes place shortly after the triumphal entry. Immediately preceding our passage, verses 28 to 40 tell the familiar story of Jesus' arrival in Jerusalem, riding from the Mount of Olives on a borrowed colt. That is a story full of drama and triumph and loud hosannas, cloaks spread on the road to make a royal welcome and also (unsurprisingly) disapproving Pharisees muttering on the sidelines. It's the climax to which this gospel has been building since chapter 9, when Jesus 'resolutely set out for Jerusalem' (Luke 9:51).

Now, straight after triumph, there is weeping. Jesus looks out over Jerusalem and speaks words of lament that echo the lamentations spoken long ago by the Old Testament prophets. Just as they bewailed Israel and Judah's indifference to their warnings, so Jesus mourns the city's failure to heed the good news that he has brought. The place of the temple, the 'Father's house', does not recognise the Lord's anointed one.

As we've already seen, the religious leaders reject Jesus' teaching. As we will reflect later this week, in doing so they influence the people to reject him too, and hosannas will become shouts of 'Crucify!' Imagine what might have happened if the 'chief priests and the teachers of the law' who met to condemn Jesus (Luke 22:66–71) had instead hailed him as Messiah.

Pray for those who lead your local church, for local councillors and for other community leaders, that God will bless them with patience, compassion and wisdom in their plans and decisions.

NAOMI STARKEY

Understanding and misunderstanding at the temple

When Jesus entered the temple courts, he began to drive out those who were selling. 'It is written,' he said to them, '"My house will be a house of prayer"; but you have made it "a den of robbers"'... [Jesus] saw the rich putting their gifts into the temple treasury. He also saw a poor widow put in two very small copper coins. 'Truly I tell you,' he said, 'this poor widow has put in more than all the others. All these people gave their gifts out of their wealth; but she out of her poverty put in all she had to live on.'

Here are two strongly contrasting scenes at the temple. First, Jesus drives out the 'sellers' to remind them of the temple's rightful purpose. Second, he draws attention to one of the poorest of the poor who makes the boldest of financial gestures. Both scenes inspire and also challenge us.

Jesus' treatment of the temple sellers sounds calculated to offend. Luke does not indicate that they were doing anything other than conducting normal business – but seeking the presence of the living God requires setting aside 'normal business'. What should our response be in terms of our local 'houses of prayer'? Close the church bookstall? Stop charging for cathedral entry? There are no easy answers.

The irony of the widow's story is that she put all her money into the very repository intended to support those in her position. Throughout the scriptures, widows are singled out as in need of special care, but this woman's generosity gives her the dignity of being able to give to others. Remember the wealthy ruler in Luke 18? Here is one of the most vulnerable members of the same society doing exactly what he could not countenance doing.

'Father, hallowed be your name, your kingdom come. Give us each day our daily bread' (Luke 11:2–3). Think about how to make more space for prayer in your local church. Think, too, about how you can learn to depend more on God for your daily needs, thus freeing yourself to bless and be blessed in giving to others.

NAOMI STARKEY

The crowds don't really understand

Every day [Jesus] was teaching at the temple. But the chief priests, the teachers of the law and the leaders among the people were trying to kill him. Yet they could not find any way to do it, because all the people hung on his words... But the whole crowd shouted, 'Away with this man! Release Barabbas to us!' (Barabbas had been thrown into prison for an insurrection in the city, and for murder.) Wanting to release Jesus, Pilate appealed to them again. But they kept shouting, 'Crucify him! Crucify him!'... So Pilate decided to grant their demand.

Here we have two violently contrasting scenes. The first follows immediately from Jesus' ejecting of the sellers from the temple. Commercial bustle has been replaced by a rapt audience, hanging on the words of the rabbi from Nazareth. The city is busy with pilgrims gathering for the Passover, many of whom would remember Jesus' dramatic entry surrounded by a cheering throng. This is the point, surely, when Jesus' authority is acclaimed on a wider stage than ever before. Even the scheming leaders seem to have been thwarted! What can possibly go wrong?

Cut to a scene just days later, at the headquarters of Pilate, the Roman governor of Judea. The crowd are baying for Jesus' blood, demanding a particularly barbaric form of execution. Maybe his supporters have been drowned out by the mob. Or perhaps the whole gathering has been orchestrated by those scheming leaders! What on earth has gone wrong?

Even though Jesus rejected the temptation of instant fame at the start of his ministry (Luke 4:5–12), now he is subjected to the brutal swing of popular mood. Over recent years social media has shown how fast adulation can turn to vilification. A film clip or photograph goes viral, spreads around the globe in a few hours, and dizzying fame – or infamy – results for the subjects. People who seek such fame or infamy should beware the personal cost; leaders who invoke 'the will of the people' should beware how fickle that 'will' can be.

Lord, keep us mindful of the risks of following the crowd,
whatever that crowd might be.

NAOMI STARKEY

Judas' tragic failure to understand

Now the Festival of Unleavened Bread, called the Passover, was approaching, and the chief priests and the teachers of the law were looking for some way to get rid of Jesus, for they were afraid of the people. Then Satan entered Judas, called Iscariot, one of the Twelve. And Judas went to the chief priests and the officers of the temple guard and discussed with them how he might betray Jesus. They were delighted and agreed to give him money. He consented, and watched for an opportunity to hand Jesus over to them when no crowd was present.

It's easy to reduce Judas to the pantomime baddie of the Easter story, playing a comparably bloodstained role to Herod at Christmas. On the other hand, mention of Satan entering Judas has led to fruitless speculation about his being 'possessed by the devil', as if Judas became a kind of horror-movie zombie, hell-bent on evil.

We don't know exactly why Judas betrayed Jesus, although that hasn't stopped the airing of many theories. Some would portray him as a disappointed freedom fighter, sacrificing his leader for failing to live up to expectations. Others consider him simply a wicked man. John's gospel takes a generally dim view of Judas, summarising him as 'a thief; as keeper of the money bag, he used to help himself to what was put into it' (John 12:6). Yet others would pity him, seeing him as the helpless puppet of God's purposes, damned so that the world might be saved.

'What could possibly go wrong?' I asked yesterday, reflecting on the crowd's eager support of Jesus. Here is the answer: one of his own followers collaborates with his enemies to isolate him from his fans and deliver him into the hands of those enemies. Judas didn't understand that he had free will, that he didn't have to listen to the voice of the accuser, the father of lies. He didn't understand – and he chose to walk in darkness instead of in the light.

Sometimes betrayal is cold-blooded deception to get the best of an opponent. Perhaps, more often, we allow betrayal to grow through half-truths, self-justifications and failing to admit our selfish motives.

NAOMI STARKEY

The disciples still don't understand

[Jesus] withdrew about a stone's throw beyond [the disciples], knelt down and prayed, 'Father, if you are willing, take this cup from me; yet not my will, but yours be done.' An angel from heaven appeared to him and strengthened him. And being in anguish, he prayed more earnestly, and his sweat was like drops of blood falling to the ground. When he rose from prayer and went back to the disciples, he found them asleep, exhausted from sorrow. 'Why are you sleeping?' he asked them. 'Get up and pray so that you will not fall into temptation.'

Jesus has eaten a last Passover with his friends; he has shared wine with them and broken bread; he has calmed a dispute as to who is the greatest; he has warned Simon Peter of that forthright disciple's inner frailty. Even so, Simon Peter does not acknowledge the truth of his Lord's words until forced by bitter circumstances to do so. He does not understand himself.

Church services on this Maundy Thursday often involve a quiet Eucharist, perhaps some foot-washing, and an hour or two of candle-lit vigil. Such traditions could end up downplaying the knife-edge uncertainty described in our passage. Jesus is 'in anguish', sweating profusely, praying earnestly – we could say desperately. Waking his sleeping disciples, he orders them to pray too, so as to escape temptation. What does he fear for them – that they will leave him? Deny him? Join Judas in siding with his enemies?

The impression is that they still don't grasp the full immensity of the events unfolding. They are 'exhausted from sorrow', perhaps troubled by Jesus' anguish, and are asleep, maybe trusting that things will be better in the morning. After all, they have two swords in case of trouble (v. 38)! They don't understand – but at least they are faithful, according to Luke. In Mark's account (14:50), every single one of them runs away.

Lord God, we may not have discovered our full strength; we may be unaware of how weak we really are. Either way, help us to know ourselves better and show us how we may best serve you, just as we are.

NAOMI STARKEY

The centurion understands

It was now about noon, and darkness came over the whole land until three in the afternoon, for the sun stopped shining. And the curtain of the temple was torn in two. Jesus called out with a loud voice, 'Father, into your hands I commit my spirit.' When he had said this, he breathed his last. The centurion, seeing what had happened, praised God and said, 'Surely this was a righteous man.' When all the people who had gathered to witness this sight saw what took place, they beat their breasts and went away.

Good Friday… and as the Son of God hangs dying, so darkness comes at noon. Luke indicates that this was a natural event – an eclipse – but it was also one of the signs of the 'day of the Lord', as described by the prophet Amos. According to Amos, the Sovereign Lord declares: 'I will make the sun go down at noon and darken the earth in broad daylight… I will make that time like mourning for an only son and the end of it like a bitter day' (Amos 8:9–10).

It is a 'bitter day' indeed, and yet God's plan for redemption is completed in Jesus' death. Matthew mentions an earthquake (Matthew 27:51–53), perhaps the trigger for the tearing of the temple curtain also mentioned by Luke. This tearing could be another example of a natural phenomenon that is powerfully symbolic, as the barriers between humanity and God are swept aside.

A centurion stands on duty, observing the brutal and strange events of that Friday afternoon – and somehow he understands. Luke's version of his declaration is less forthright than Mark's – where he says, 'Surely this man was the Son of God!' (Mark 15:39) – but still shows clearly that this Gentile, this member of the occupying military force, sees that here was no ordinary criminal or rebel suffering a cruel death. This was 'a righteous man'.

The crowd see what has happened and express their grief and regret – too late to make a difference. Let us pray to be so attuned to God's purposes in the world that we understand more often than we misunderstand.

NAOMI STARKEY

Joseph of Arimathea understands

Now there was a man named Joseph, a member of the Council, a good and upright man, who had not consented to their decision and action. He came from the Judean town of Arimathea, and he himself was waiting for the kingdom of God. Going to Pilate, he asked for Jesus' body. Then he took it down, wrapped it in linen cloth and placed it in a tomb cut in the rock, one in which no one had yet been laid. It was Preparation Day, and the Sabbath was about to begin.

Here's a shock: Joseph is a council member, a key figure in the religious establishment, whose distance from their scheming against Jesus is spelled out clearly. He also appears in John's gospel as 'a disciple of Jesus, but secretly because he feared the Jewish leaders', and in that account of Jesus' death, he does the work of burial with Nicodemus, who had 'visited Jesus at night' (John 19:38–39).

Thanks to the social and religious standing of these men, Jesus is buried with a level of reverence and respect that would not normally have been accorded to a criminal after public execution. Note the detail that the tomb had not been used for any other interments. This is not just a matter of its being a fitting place for the Lord to lie, but to underline the fact that there could be no mix-up as to which body had gone missing on Easter morning. There had only ever been one body in that tomb – the body of Jesus.

Disciples (whether secret or not) are needed in positions of power and influence in society. They can use their power and influence to do good deeds, which may run counter to the values of that society, while not casting those disciples in the role of revolutionaries. Those whose calling it is to campaign on the front line against injustice, at whatever cost to themselves, should refrain from judging those who work behind the scenes.

Father in heaven, keep us from trying to be what we are not,
out of dissatisfaction with who we are. May we understand and accept
whom you have created and called us to be.

NAOMI STARKEY

Understanding dawns for all

On the first day of the week, very early in the morning, the women took the spices they had prepared and went to the tomb. They found the stone rolled away from the tomb, but when they entered, they did not find the body of the Lord Jesus. While they were wondering about this, suddenly two men in clothes that gleamed like lightning stood beside them. In their fright the women bowed down with their faces to the ground, but the men said to them, 'Why do you look for the living among the dead? He is not here; he has risen!'

At last, it is the day of resurrection, the third day after Jesus was delivered 'to the hands of sinners [and] crucified' (v. 7). But the women coming to the tomb – including Mary Magdalene, Joanna and Mary the mother of James – do not remember Jesus' promise of being 'raised again' until the men in shining clothes remind them (v. 8).

Remembering does not necessarily equate to believing, however. Luke tells how they go to the remaining eleven of the inner circle of disciples and report what has happened (presumably also repeating Jesus' promise). The reaction is that they are judged to be speaking 'nonsense' (v. 11), although Peter does make a trip to the tomb, finds it empty and puzzles over the possible implications. Could Jesus have been speaking the truth about himself all along?

In the end, the light of understanding dawns for him and for the rest of the disciples. On the day of Pentecost, the fire of the Spirit (Acts 2:3) ignites their hearts with courage and gives them the words to begin sharing with the whole world God's plan of salvation. As the apostle Paul wrote a few years later: 'We declare God's wisdom, a mystery that has been hidden and that God destined for our glory before time began' (1 Corinthians 2:7).

Our faith rests in a mystery – but a revealed mystery. We believe and trust in God incarnate, not a remote nameless deity. Understanding these truths is the task of a lifetime; salvation, meanwhile, is God's gift to us.

Lord, I believe; help me overcome my unbelief (see Mark 9:24).

NAOMI STARKEY

Lent study questions

How to use this material in a group

Traditionally, most readers of *New Daylight* use the notes and reflections as part of their individual study and, of course, this Lent booklet can be used in this way. The readings and reflections are set out in the usual way, so that the rhythm of daily prayer and study can be continued. Those who are using *New Daylight* for the first time will find all they need within this booklet to begin a habit of daily encounter with God that will build them up in their faith and encourage them on their journey.

Additional material has also been provided so that those who wish to can meet together to share their Lent studies and insights. Questions have been written by the authors of each set of reflections, which relate both to the material for each day and to the whole week's worth of readings.

The suggested timetable is for meetings to take place during the week *after* the date of the readings in question, and the questions are therefore arranged so that groups can begin during the week of Ash Wednesday (that is, the week commencing Sunday 3 March), looking at the material for the week commencing Sunday 24 February. The final group meeting is after Easter Sunday and can be held that week or the following week. In this way, we encourage people to think about what comes next; the story didn't end at Easter.

This material can be used in a number of different ways by all sorts of groups. It can form the basis for a weekly Lent group or provide topics of discussion at Lent lunches or suppers. It can be used as conversation starters for groups that already meet, such as midweek fellowship groups, Mothers' Union meetings or men's breakfasts.

If a new group is beginning, it is a good idea to include refreshments with each meeting – some groups find an evening meal with discussion round the table very popular, while others feel that drinks and biscuits or cake are more appropriate. This kind of hospitality can break down barriers and introduce people to each other in a relaxed way, which in turn will lead to a livelier, more fruitful discussion.

Remember to provide prospective members of the group with booklets well before the beginning of Lent. The reflections begin before Ash Wednesday and they will provide a useful way into the style of *New Daylight* before the meetings begin.

Suggestions for group meetings

The group leader may or may not also be the group host. Either or both of these roles may be fixed for the whole of Lent or rotate among the group.

If the group leader and host are different people, they should liaise beforehand to ensure arrangements are in place, the time and date are fixed and refreshments are available.

Introduction Make sure each person has a copy of the booklet and that spares are available for those who do not. Introduce newcomers to the group and make them feel welcome. Remind everyone that they do not have to contribute to the discussion if they don't want to, but that conversation will be livelier if they do!

Opening prayer Use a prayer within the traditions of the group; this will help put people at ease, and those who are familiar with the traditions will lend confidence to those who are not. A song or hymn can be sung.

Discussion If the group is large, split into twos or threes to discuss reactions to the week's reflections. Allow time for each person to share, if they wish. If discussion is slow to start, suggest that each member offers one word or sentence that sums up their reaction.

Forum As one group, try to discern some themes that are common to most members. If it helps, write these down and circulate them among the group.

Reflection Study the group questions, and spend some time in silence so that individuals can reflect on the theme personally. Come together to discuss the questions. Again, if the group is large it is helpful to split into smaller groups.

Plenary The leader draws together the themes arising from the discussion, and sees whether they mirror those from the week's reflections. Again, these can be noted for later distribution.

Prayer It can be helpful to begin your prayer time with silence, in order to meditate on the results of the discussion. This can be followed by open prayer. Be flexible, allowing time for each person to contribute if they wish.

Closing prayer.

Contemplative prayer

MARGARET SILF

Suggested meeting date: week commencing 3 March

- Is there a physical space, either in your home or in the natural world, that helps to draw your deepest centre into orbit around God?

- Spend some time 'basking in the light' of God's love. How easy is this for you to do and what difficulties do you encounter? How do you feel afterwards?

- Take time this week to gaze into the heart of a plant, a tree or any other natural object, and see the wonder that is hidden inside it. Can you now apply this wisdom to those people who live alongside you – family, friends, colleagues, neighbours? Can you look into the mirror and apply this wisdom to yourself?

- Where and how do you draw upon the deep oceans of life that sustain you through the dry periods of your life?

- When you are feeling anxious or exhausted, where do you go to soak up the refreshing dew?

- When and where have you experienced 'timeless moments'?

- Have you ever been 'in a hard place' and discovered that God was there, even if you didn't realise it at the time?

Group questions

- As you look back over the past seven days, did you find any time simply to 'gaze on God' and let God's light shine upon you?

- Can you make this part of your regular spiritual practice?

- What personal challenges might you encounter in trying to do so?

For your notes

Contemplative prayer

MARGARET SILF

Suggested meeting date: week commencing 10 March

- Can you recall any times in your own life when you have felt 'emptied out'? In hindsight, can you see how God used that emptiness to lead you to a new level of fullness?

- How do you see your own inner Martha and inner Mary? How do you feel about the balance between them? Do your reflections reveal anything you would wish to adjust in your own priorities?

- What form does your own 'well of contemplation' take?

- What does the 'secret place' mean for you, in practice? How might you make contemplative prayer a part of your Lenten practice?

- When you pray, can you let the seed of your longing fall into God's heart and trust God to grow it for you, or do you feel you need to give God the growing instructions?

- Have you ever stayed in the silence at the still centre of a stormy conflict? How did that feel, and what was the effect?

- What are the challenges for you in 'staying awake'?

Group questions

- What has struck you most about the reflections of the past two weeks?

- Is there anything that you would now wish to make part of your ongoing spiritual practice?

For your notes

Place

LIZ HOARE

Suggested meeting date: week commencing 17 March

- Is there a place you can return to, perhaps in your memory, where you first called on the name of the Lord and found clarity for the road ahead?

- What should we make of Jacob's prayer in Genesis 32:26? If we find ourselves in a place where we are echoing Jacob's words, are we prepared to face the cost involved as well as the reward?

- Have you ever had an experience like Moses did at Horeb? What do you think it meant?

- Can you recall a wilderness experience where you knew that God was sustaining you? Can you find a metaphor to describe this?

- What things are important for you to remember, and what 'memory stones' help you to do so?

- If God asked you, 'What are you doing here?', how would you answer?

- Have you ever resisted God's call because you felt unworthy? How does Isaiah's experience in the temple help you to be more ready to go?

Group questions

- Which of the places this week has spoken to you most deeply?

- Why do you think certain places echo our spiritual experiences?

For your notes

Place

LIZ HOARE

Suggested meeting date: week commencing 24 March

- What have you learned when it seems that nothing is happening?

- 'Follow me': what does that involve for you today?

- How does the image of living water speak to your needs?

- What places and situations seem dark and without hope? How could you pray for them to be transfigured?

- Is 'friend' a name you often use to address Jesus? What difference could it make to your praying to call him 'friend'?

- How often do you pray 'Your will be done' as a prayer of trust rather than as a way of opting out of being specific?

- Is there anything in Jesus' teaching during his earthly ministry that would lead us to expect his response to the thief's request on the cross?

Group questions

- What has surprised you about places and their significance in the life of Jesus on earth?

- Are there places in your life story that bring to mind something Jesus said about himself? Where are these places and what was it about them that spoke to you about the Lord?

For your notes

Exile

MICHAEL MITTON

Suggested meeting date: week commencing 31 March

- What do you feel as you read about the exile from Eden?

- Do you find it easy to express your laments to God? What do you think he feels about them?

- As you look back at your journey with God, what memories feel like empowering memories?

- How could an exile experience cause you to see a new vision of God?

- How have your experiences of exile changed your view of God?

- When we experience an exile of any kind, what do we need to help us choose love over self-pity?

- How does being a citizen of the kingdom of heaven affect how you live in this world?

Group questions

- What types of exile have you experienced/are you experiencing in life? What has been particularly difficult about them? How did you manage/are you managing them? Where has God been for you in each situation? Give time for each person to tell his or her story.

- How easy do you find it to express your laments to God? Think about how you do this personally and also together with others in corporate worship. Can you think of ways of doing lament better? How can lament (both personal and corporate) be therapeutic and faith-building?

- We have been reading about the power of memory, presence, hope and love in exile. Which of these have been significant for you and why? Are any of these particularly difficult?

For your notes

Exile

MICHAEL MITTON

Suggested meeting date: week commencing 7 April

- What do you feel about this image of the Spirit of God being the dove, whose natural habitat is the wilderness?

- Who might be the equivalent of the centurion for you? Can you see signs of faith in their heart?

- What is the equivalent of Caesarea Philippi for you? How might Christ be revealed in such a place?

- What imprisons you? When you feel trapped or imprisoned, try starting to praise and worship God from your heart.

- How do you view your body? How do you imagine the resurrection body that Paul describes in 1 Corinthians 15?

- How hard do you think it was for Jesus to feel at home in this world? What are the characteristics of his homeland?

- What difference does it make to you today to know that God yearns to dwell fully in your company?

Group questions

- What sort of life experiences have felt like a wilderness to you? Has God felt close or absent at such times? How do you think the Spirit might help us to feel at home in a wilderness place?

- What might be a modern-day equivalent of Caesarea Philippi? What would a church founded in that place look like? What might be a sign of the gates of Hades giving way?

- In the final two readings, we discover a God who delights in making himself at home among humans. Is this how you see God? What is there about your church that you think God would like and would make him feel at home? How does John's vision in Revelation 21 affect how you live today?

For your notes

To Calvary and beyond

NAOMI STARKEY

Suggested meeting date: week commencing 14 April

- Which is harder to endure – physical or mental pain – and why?
- What more can your church(es) do to welcome little children?
- Have you – or somebody you know – had a life-changing encounter that you can share with the group?
- In what practical ways can you show something of God's astonishing generosity in your local community?
- What would you find hardest to sacrifice in answering God's call to service – and why?
- What are the risks of popular acclaim for those in church leadership?
- Share your experiences as a group of sensing God's presence in a place of pilgrimage (or your regular place of worship).

Group questions

- How much (honestly!) do you feel you know about what it means to be a follower of Jesus? Who are the outsiders in your community who need to hear the good news of God's kingdom?
- The disciples so often failed to understand the implications of Jesus' teaching, despite their closeness to him. To what extent might the church today be at risk of failing to understand?

For your notes

To Calvary and beyond

NAOMI STARKEY

Suggested meeting date: week commencing 21 April

- Can you think of examples of national leaders who have acted decisively for good, even if at personal cost?

- What impression of your church's priorities would a visitor receive from the building?

- Could the negative effects of social media outweigh the positives?

- How hard is it to rebuild trust after betrayal? Are there times when it is impossible?

- What part does Maundy Thursday play in your experience of Holy Week?

- Have you sensed God at work (or communicating) through natural phenomena? What are the possibilities – and pitfalls – of looking for such 'signs'?

- How might church members use their personal positions in the community – in both working and leisure hours – to spread the ways of God's kingdom?

- How do you deal with your doubts about God, faith and the church?

Group questions

- Which are better attended in your church – Christmas or Easter services? Is there a balance that needs redressing?

- Which of the different characters in the Easter story resonate most with you – and why?

- Do we have to hold back on joy till Easter morning, or is it appropriate to be glad on Good Friday too?

For your notes

Next steps

We have reached Easter Sunday, the climax of our Lenten journey. However, we have not yet arrived at our real destination, because although we have studied and read and reflected and practised for over 40 days, we are not at the very end. The wonder of the empty tomb must continue to send its echoes into our daily lives, as we take up the message it sings to us and sing it in our turn, accompanying our journey with the hymns of redemption and the choruses of salvation. The journey of faith is as long as the journey of our lives, ending only when we arrive at our eternal home, prepared so lovingly for us by Christ, who has gone before us for that very purpose.

Hopefully, the practices of Lent, the disciplines of daily study and reflection, and the structures of prayer and contemplation will have been put in place and, through the steady repetition of the last 40 days, will have become a habit, part of the fabric of our daily lives. However, it is not enough merely to establish a habit – that habit must be kept up if it is to accomplish its purpose.

As we continue beyond Easter, we look for the promises of Pentecost and take upon ourselves the great commission as we continue to explore all that the suffering, death and resurrection of Christ mean for us and for the world.

My prayers are for you as you continue on your journey.

Questions for the next stage of the journey

- What have I learned about myself during this Lenten period?

- What have I learned about God?

- Which spiritual practices have been new to me? How useful have I found them?

- What do I need to do to sustain a practice of prayer and reflection?

Exercises

Draw a map of your spiritual journey. Using pictures or words, write or illustrate the high points and the low ones you have experienced in your relationship with God. You might want to think about times of faith and doubt, times when God has revealed his presence to you and times when it has seemed he was absent. Picture yourself at the beginning of a new stage – what are you looking towards? Where do you hope to be?

Find pictures of roads or paths, and keep them in your prayer space or as bookmarks for your Bible. Use the pictures to remind you to pray for yourself on your journey, asking God for the grace to 'run with perseverance the race that is set before us, looking to Jesus the pioneer and perfecter of our faith' (Hebrews 12:1–2, NRSV).

If you don't already do so, consider keeping a prayer journal. In this, you can keep a note not only of your prayers for yourself and others, but also of the occasions of answered prayers and times of spiritual refreshment and joy. This can serve as both a record of answered prayer and a source of comfort and hope when times are challenging.

How to encourage Bible reading in your church

BRF has been helping individuals connect with the Bible for over 90 years. We want to support churches as they seek to encourage church members into regular Bible reading.

Order a Bible reading resources pack

This pack is designed to give your church the tools to publicise our Bible reading notes. It includes:

- Sample Bible reading notes for your congregation to try.
- Publicity resources, including a poster.
- A church magazine feature about Bible reading notes.

The pack is free, but we welcome a £5 donation to cover the cost of postage. If you require a pack to be sent outside the UK or require a specific number of sample Bible reading notes, please contact us for postage costs. More information about what the current pack contains is available on our website.

How to order and find out more

- Visit **biblereadingnotes.org.uk/for-churches**
- Telephone BRF on **+44 (0)1865 319700** Mon–Fri 9.15–17.30
- Write to us at BRF, 15 The Chambers, Vineyard, Abingdon OX14 3FE

Keep informed about our latest initiatives

We are continuing to develop resources to help churches encourage people into regular Bible reading, wherever they are on their journey. Join our email list at **brfonline.org.uk/signup** to stay informed about the latest initiatives that your church could benefit from.

NEW DAYLIGHT SUBSCRIPTION RATES

Please note our subscription rates, current until **30 April 2019**:

Individual subscriptions
covering 3 issues for under 5 copies, payable in advance
(including postage & packing):

	UK	Europe	Rest of world
New Daylight	£16.95	£25.20	£29.10
New Daylight 3-year subscription (9 issues) (not available for Deluxe)	£46.35	N/A	N/A
New Daylight Deluxe per set of 3 issues p.a.	£21.45	£32.25	£38.25

Group subscriptions
covering 3 issues for 5 copies or more, sent to **one** UK address (post free):

New Daylight	£13.50 per set of 3 issues p.a.
New Daylight Deluxe	£17.25 per set of 3 issues p.a.

Please note that the annual billing period for group subscriptions runs from 1 May to 30 April.

Overseas group subscription rates
Available on request. Please email **enquiries@brf.org.uk**.

Copies may also be obtained from Christian bookshops:

New Daylight	£4.50 per copy
New Daylight Deluxe	£5.75 per copy
Lent with New Daylight	£2.99 per copy

All our Bible reading notes can be ordered online by visiting
biblereadingnotes.org.uk/subscriptions

For information about our other Bible reading notes,
and apps for iPhone and iPod touch, visit
biblereadingnotes.org.uk

NEW DAYLIGHT INDIVIDUAL SUBSCRIPTION FORM

All our Bible reading notes can be ordered online by visiting
biblereadingnotes.org.uk/subscriptions

☐ I would like to take out a subscription:

Title .... First name/initials .... Surname ....

Address ....

.... Postcode ....

Telephone .... Email ....

Please send *New Daylight* beginning with the January 2019 / May 2019 / September 2019 issue (*delete as appropriate*):

(*please tick box*)

	UK	Europe	Rest of world
New Daylight 1-year subscription	☐ £16.95	☐ £25.20	☐ £29.10
New Daylight 3-year subscription	☐ £46.35	N/A	N/A
New Daylight Deluxe	☐ £21.45	☐ £32.25	☐ £38.25

Total enclosed £ .... (cheques should be made payable to 'BRF')

Please charge my MasterCard / Visa ☐ Debit card ☐ with £ ....

Card no. ☐☐☐☐ ☐☐☐☐ ☐☐☐☐ ☐☐☐☐

Valid from ☐☐/☐☐ Expires ☐☐/☐☐ Security code* ☐☐☐

Last 3 digits on the reverse of the card

Signature* .... Date ..../......./.......

*ESSENTIAL IN ORDER TO PROCESS YOUR PAYMENT

To set up a Direct Debit, please also complete the Direct Debit instruction on page 96 and return it to BRF with this form.

Please return this form with the appropriate payment to:
BRF, 15 The Chambers, Vineyard, Abingdon OX14 3FE

To read our terms and find out about cancelling your order, please visit **brfonline.org.uk/terms**.

The Bible Reading Fellowship is a Registered Charity (233280)

LWND2019

DIRECT DEBIT PAYMENT

You can pay for your annual subscription to our Bible reading notes using Direct Debit. You need only give your bank details once, and the payment is made automatically every year until you cancel it. If you would like to pay by Direct Debit, please use the form overleaf, entering your BRF account number under 'Reference number'.

You are fully covered by the Direct Debit Guarantee:

The Direct Debit Guarantee

- This Guarantee is offered by all banks and building societies that accept instructions to pay Direct Debits.

- If there are any changes to the amount, date or frequency of your Direct Debit, The Bible Reading Fellowship will notify you 10 working days in advance of your account being debited or as otherwise agreed. If you request The Bible Reading Fellowship to collect a payment, confirmation of the amount and date will be given to you at the time of the request.

- If an error is made in the payment of your Direct Debit, by The Bible Reading Fellowship or your bank or building society, you are entitled to a full and immediate refund of the amount paid from your bank or building society.

- If you receive a refund you are not entitled to, you must pay it back when The Bible Reading Fellowship asks you to.

- You can cancel a Direct Debit at any time by simply contacting your bank or building society. Written confirmation may be required. Please also notify us.

The Bible Reading Fellowship

Instruction to your bank or building society to pay by Direct Debit

Please fill in the whole form using a ballpoint pen and return it to:
BRF, 15 The Chambers, Vineyard, Abingdon OX14 3FE

Service User Number:

5	5	8	2	2	9

Name and full postal address of your bank or building society

To: The Manager	Bank/Building Society
Address	
	Postcode

Name(s) of account holder(s)

Branch sort code

		–			–		

Bank/Building Society account number

Reference number

Instruction to your Bank/Building Society
Please pay The Bible Reading Fellowship Direct Debits from the account detailed
in this instruction, subject to the safeguards assured by the Direct Debit Guarantee. I understand
that this instruction may remain with The Bible Reading Fellowship and, if so, details will be
passed electronically to my bank/building society.

Signature(s)

Banks and Building Societies may not accept Direct Debit instructions for some types of account.

LWND2019